THE GLOBAL CITIZEN'S HANDBOOK
FACING OUR WORLD'S CRISES AND CHALLENGES

Collins
An Imprint of HarperCollinsPublishers

THE WORLD BANK
Washington, D.C.

www.harpercollins.com

ISBN: 978-0-06-124342-4
ISBN-10: 0-06-124342-6

FIRST U.S. EDITION Published in 2007.

HarperCollins books may be purchased
for educational, business, or sales promotional use. For
information in the United States, please write to:
Special Markets Department, HarperCollins Publishers,
10 East 53rd Street, New York, NY 10022.

Text © The International Bank for Reconstruction and Development / The World Bank, 2007

Designed by Collins UK

Printed and bound by Imago, Singapore

10 09 08 07
7 6 5 4 3 2

Contents

Acknowledgements

The text and data of *The Global Citizen's Handbook* were prepared by the Development Data Group of the World Bank under the management of Shaida Badiee. The team consisted of Mehdi Akhlaghi, Uranbileg Batjargal, David Cieslikowski, Mahyar Eshragh-Tabary, Richard Fix, Amy Heyman, Masako Hiraga, Raymond Muhula, Sulekha Patel, William Prince, Changqing Sun, Eric Swanson, and K. M. Vijayalakshmi. Sebastien Dessus, Shahrokh Fardoust, Jeff Lecksell, Jeff Lewis, M. H. Saeed Ordoubadi, and Giovanni Ruta made valuable contributions. Denise Bergeron, Valentina Kalk, Stephen McGroarty, and Santiago Pombo from the World Bank's Office of the Publisher oversaw publication and dissemination of the book.

The Publishing, Design, Editorial, Creative Services, and Database teams at Collins Reference, HarperCollins Publishers, provided overall design direction, editorial control, mapping, and DTP origination.

Picture credits

Curt Carnemark/World Bank 10, 14, 20, 22, 30, 68, 84, 106, 108, 117, 118; **Kevin Coombs/Reuters/ Corbis** 86; **Francis Dobbs/World Bank** 80; **Douglas Engle/Corbis** 111 (top); **J. Emilio Flores/Corbis** 36; **Alan Ginoux/World Bank** 82; **Masuru Goto/World Bank** 56; **Louise Gubb/Corbis** 102; **Yosef Hadar/ World Bank** 18; **Collart Herve/Corbis Sygma** 93; **Tran Thi Hoa/World Bank** 52; **Arne Hoel/World Bank** 71; **Anvar Ilyasov/World Bank** 100; **Ed Kashi/Corbis** 76; **Kazuyoshi/Corbis** 114; **Bob Krist/ Corbis** 24; **Frans Lanting/Corbis** 112; **Bill Lyons/World Bank** 64; **Stephanie Maze/Corbis** 96; **Gideon Mendel/Corbis** 59 (bottom); **Eric Miller/World Bank** 63, 72, 89 (top); **Viviane Moos/Corbis** 89 (bottom), 94; **Stephen Morrison/epa/Corbis** 74; **Shehzad Noorani/World Bank** 54; **Charles O'Rear/Corbis** 75; **Anatoliy Rakhimbayev/World Bank** 99, 105; **Gennadiy Ratushenko/World Bank** 44; **Reuters/Corbis** 33; **Trevor Samson/World Bank** 13, 40; **Dominic Sansoni/World Bank** 79; **Alfredo Srur/World Bank** 48; **Shannon Stapleton/Reuters/Corbis** 34; **Eberhard Streichan/Zefa/Corbis** 120; **Wendy Stone/Corbis** 26; **William Taufic/Corbis** 59 (top); **UNEP** 111 (bottom); **Ami Vitale/World Bank** 39; **Scott Wallace/World Bank** 60; **Ray Witlin/World Bank** 47, 51; **Adam Woolfitt/Corbis** 90.

Foreword

Development is a multidimensional process characterized by economic growth, investment and technological progress, transformation of natural resources, demographic change, advances in health and education, and evolution of social and political institutions. The results of development should be measurable by increases in output, improvements in the welfare of people, greater efficiency in the use of scarce resources, and a balance between human needs and the capacity of the environment to provide for those needs.

Because development is a complex process, it cannot be measured by a single yardstick. Simply measuring the size of an economy or its rate of growth tells us little about who benefited from growth, whether they are better educated and healthier, or if the air, water, and land around them have been degraded. Furthermore, there is no simple or unique path to development. Countries have different endowments and different opportunities. Some have first developed their agricultural sectors and then industrialized; others with great mineral wealth have remained primary commodity producers; and some are rapidly developing their service sectors. Export-led growth is a recent prescription for development, but small countries have always needed to trade for the goods and services they need, while large countries with large hinterlands can remain more self-sufficient.

Development is a process that never ends. We speak loosely of developed and developing countries, but no country or society ever stops developing. Rich countries as well as poor countries face the challenge of meeting their current needs while ensuring that future generations inherit a better and more productive world. Statistics, it has been said, are the eyes of the policy maker. They are also the eyes of citizens. Through them we can see development in action. We can identify places of great need, we can set goals for improvement, and we can measure success or take stock of failures. Statistics, therefore, are an important means of enforcing accountability on governments, businesses, and other actors.

To be useful, statistics must be reliable. And to help us understand the global process of development, they must be comparable across countries and over time. This book seeks to provide a comprehensive picture of the world's development at the beginning of the 21st century. It draws on the large set of statistical indicators that have been collected by the World Bank to guide its development programs. These indicators come from many sources. Most have been collected by agencies of the United Nations and shared by them as part of their mandate to increase knowledge and understanding. But all have their origins in work carried out in countries, usually by statistical offices or other public agencies, sometimes under very adverse conditions, in order to provide the basic information needed to manage their economies and provide services to their citizens.

We hope that readers of this book will find it informative, that it will expand their view of the world. And that they will recognize both the formidable challenges and the great successes that have been achieved in creating a better world for all.

François Bourguignon
Senior Vice President and Chief Economist
World Bank

Classification of economies

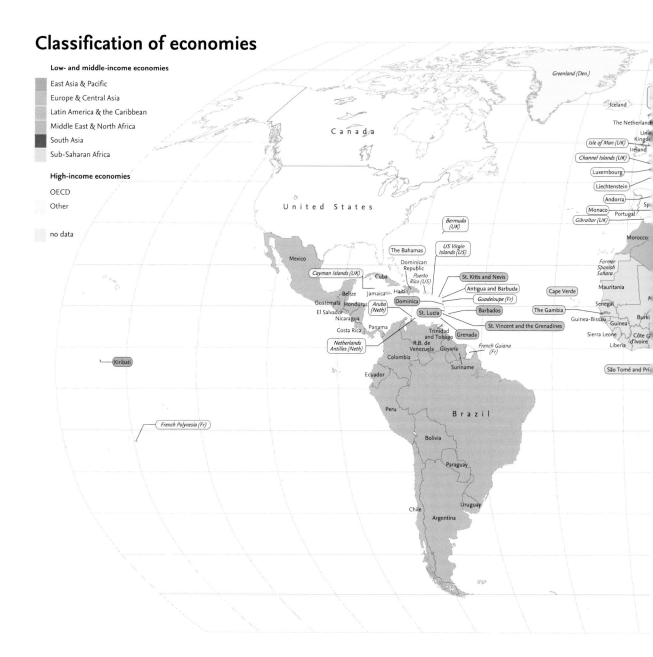

Low- and middle-income economies

- East Asia & Pacific
- Europe & Central Asia
- Latin America & the Caribbean
- Middle East & North Africa
- South Asia
- Sub-Saharan Africa

High-income economies

- OECD
- Other

no data

The World Bank classifies economies as low income, middle income (subdivided into lower middle and upper middle), or high income based on gross national income (GNI) per capita. Low- and middle-income economies are sometimes referred to as developing economies. It is not intended to imply that all economies in the group are experiencing similar development or that other economies have reached a preferred or final stage of development.

The regions used in this atlas are based on the regions defined by the World Bank for

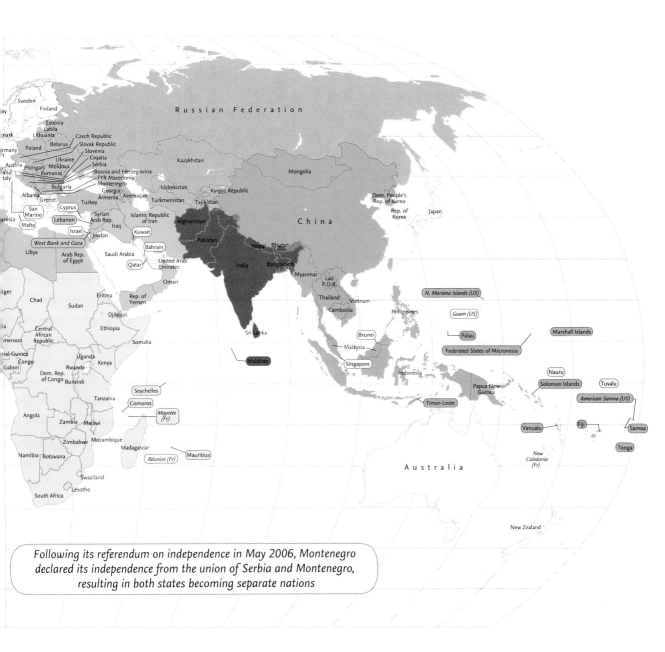

Following its referendum on independence in May 2006, Montenegro declared its independence from the union of Serbia and Montenegro, resulting in both states becoming separate nations

analytical and operational purposes. These regions may differ from common geographic usage or from the regions defined by other organizations. Regional groupings and the aggregate measures for regions include only low- and middle-income economies.

Data are shown for economies as they were constituted in 2005. Additional information about the data is provided in *World Development Indicators 2006* or on the World Bank website (www.worldbank.org/data).

There are large differences in standards of living across the globe. Gross national income (GNI) per capita, which measures the average income of residents of an economy, ranges from a few hundred dollars a year in the poorest countries to more than $40,000 a year in the richest. Although 85 percent of the world's population live in developing countries, their residents received about 46 percent of global income in 2005.

What is a developing country? Because development encompasses many factors —economic, environmental, cultural, educational, institutional—no single measure gives a complete picture. However, the total output of an country, measured by its gross national income (GNI), is a good measure of its capacity to provide for the well-being of its people. Therefore the World Bank classifies countries according to their average income, their GNI per capita. Countries with average incomes of less than $10,725 in 2005 are classified as *developing* (often referred to as low- and middle-income economies). Countries with average incomes of $10,726 or more in 2005 are classified as *developed* (often referred to as high-income economies). In 2005, the 1 billion people in high-income economies had an average income of $35,130, while the 5.4 billion people in developing economies earned $1,750 per capita. The differences among developing economies are also large. The 3.1 billion residents in economies classified as middle-income had an average income of $2,640, while the 2.4 billion people in low-income economies earned only $580 on average, with some earning as little as $100 a person per year.

Comparisons of income between economies need to take into account differences

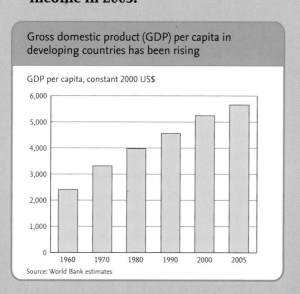

Gross domestic product (GDP) per capita in developing countries has been rising

GDP per capita, constant 2000 US$

Source: World Bank estimates

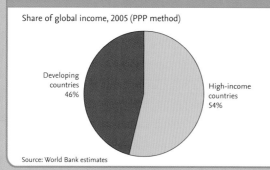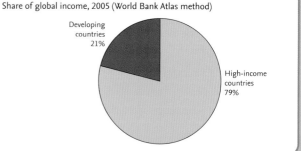

Comparing income measures—Purchasing power parity (PPP) vs exchange rates: The share of developing countries' gross national income as a share of global income is twice as much measured with the PPP method than with exchange rates.

Share of global income, 2005 (PPP method)

Developing countries 46%

High-income countries 54%

Share of global income, 2005 (World Bank Atlas method)

Developing countries 21%

High-income countries 79%

Source: World Bank estimates

in exchange rates and the price levels. This is done using purchasing power parities (PPPs). Measured using PPPs, developing economies receive 46 percent of world income. But when measured using three-year average exchange rates (World Bank Atlas method), which reflect the values of currencies in world markets, they earn only 21 percent of world income. The difference is due to the lower cost of non-traded goods and services in developing economies, a fact that travelers frequently observe.

As the most comprehensive measure of living standards, GNI per capita is closely related to other, non-monetary, measures of the quality of life, such as life expectancy at birth, the mortality rate of children, and enrollment rates in school. Low incomes are both a cause and effect of low levels of health, education, and other human development outcomes: poor people have a hard time obtaining good health care and education, while poor health and poor education leave them less able to improve their incomes.

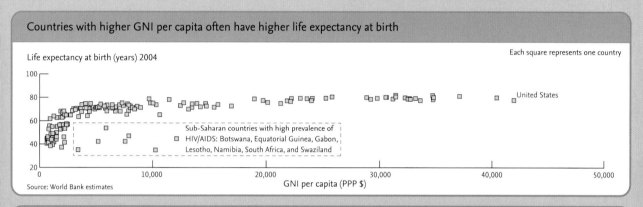
Countries with higher GNI per capita often have higher life expectancy at birth

Life expectancy at birth (years) 2004

Each square represents one country

Sub-Saharan countries with high prevalence of HIV/AIDS: Botswana, Equatorial Guinea, Gabon, Lesotho, Namibia, South Africa, and Swaziland

United States

GNI per capita (PPP $)

Source: World Bank estimates

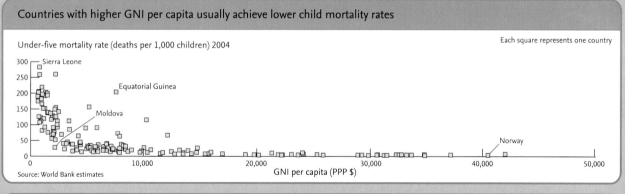
Countries with higher GNI per capita usually achieve lower child mortality rates

Under-five mortality rate (deaths per 1,000 children) 2004

Each square represents one country

Sierra Leone
Equatorial Guinea
Moldova
Norway

GNI per capita (PPP $)

Source: World Bank estimates

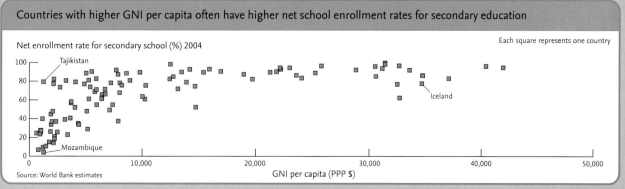
Countries with higher GNI per capita often have higher net school enrollment rates for secondary education

Net enrollment rate for secondary school (%) 2004

Each square represents one country

Tajikistan
Iceland
Mozambique

GNI per capita (PPP $)

Source: World Bank estimates

Income

GNI per capita, World Bank Atlas method, 2005

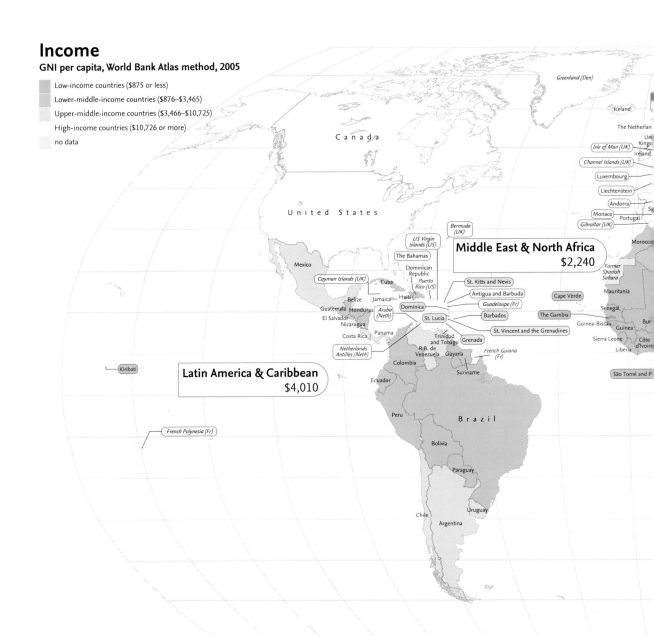

- Low-income countries ($875 or less)
- Lower-middle-income countries ($876–$3,465)
- Upper-middle-income countries ($3,466–$10,725)
- High-income countries ($10,726 or more)
- no data

Middle East & North Africa
$2,240

Latin America & Caribbean
$4,010

Greenland (Den)

Iceland

The Netherlan

Un
Kingc
Isle of Man (UK) Ireland

Channel Islands (UK)

Luxembourg

Liechtenstein

Andorra

Monaco Portugal

Gibraltar (UK)

Canada

United States

Morocco

Former
Spanish
Sahara

Mauritania

Cape Verde Senegal

The Gambia

Guinea-Bissau Guinea Bur

Sierra Leone Côte
d'Ivoire

Liberia

São Tomé and P

*Bermuda
(UK)*

*US Virgin
Islands (US)*

The Bahamas

Mexico

Dominican
Republic

Cayman Islands (UK) Cuba *Puerto
Rico (US)*

Belize Jamaica Haiti

Guatemala Honduras *Aruba
(Neth)* Dominica

El Salvador

Nicaragua

St. Kitts and Nevis

Antigua and Barbuda

Guadeloupe (Fr)

St. Lucia Barbados

St. Vincent and the Grenadines

Costa Rica Panama

*Netherlands
Antilles (Neth)*

Trinidad
and Tobago Grenada

R.B. de
Venezuela Guyana *French Guiana
(Fr)*

Colombia Suriname

Ecuador

Kiribati

Peru Brazil

French Polynesia (Fr)

Bolivia

Paraguay

Chile Uruguay

Argentina

Living conditions in Liberia, one of the world's poorest countries

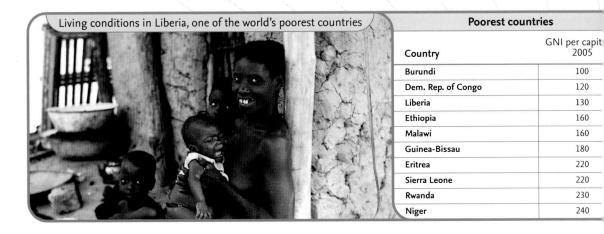

Poorest countries

Country	GNI per capit 2005
Burundi	100
Dem. Rep. of Congo	120
Liberia	130
Ethiopia	160
Malawi	160
Guinea-Bissau	180
Eritrea	220
Sierra Leone	220
Rwanda	230
Niger	240

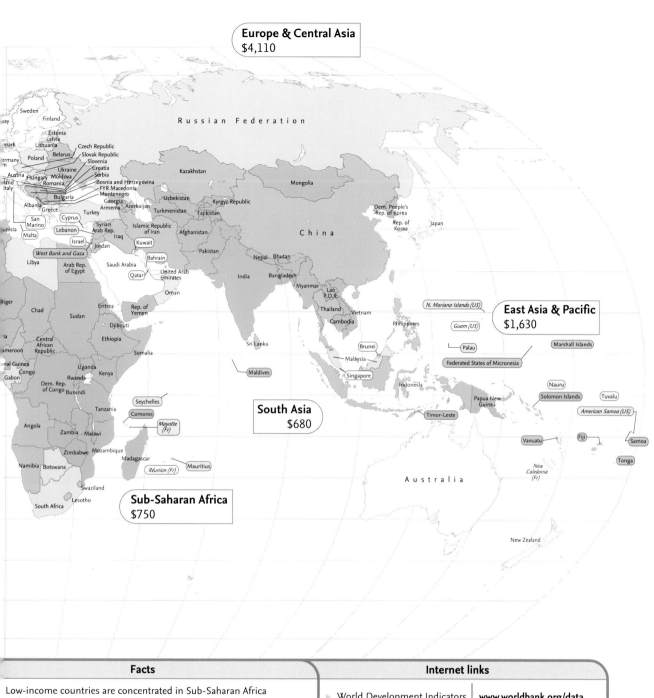

Europe & Central Asia
$4,110

East Asia & Pacific
$1,630

South Asia
$680

Sub-Saharan Africa
$750

Facts	Internet links	
Low-income countries are concentrated in Sub-Saharan Africa and Asia.	▷ World Development Indicators	**www.worldbank.org/data**
Of the poorest 40 countries, 29 are in Sub-Saharan Africa, 10 are in Asia, and one is in Latin America and Caribbean.	▷ OECD Statistics	**www.oecd.org/statistics**
Most economies in Latin America and the Caribbean, Europe and Central Asia, and the Middle East and North Africa regions are middle-income.	▷ United Nations System of National Accounts	**unstats.un.org/unsd/ nationalaccount/nasp.htm**
Variations within each region can also be large. For example, in 2005 Botswana's GNI per capita surpassed $5,000, while its neighbor Zimbabwe's GNI per capita was only $340.	▷ IMF Dissemination Standards Bulletin Board	**dsbb.imf.org/Applications/ web/dsbbhome**
Since 1989, 16 economies have moved from developing to high-income status and four high-income economies have been re-classified to developing country status.	▷ International Comparison Project	**www.worldbank.org/data/icp**

Faster growth in developing economies since 1990 is reducing poverty rates and slowly closing the income gap with high-income countries. But gains from economic growth are often not distributed evenly. To promote broad-based growth, people must be empowered and have the opportunity to make choices that improve their well-being.

Sustained growth is essential to reduce poverty, but not many developing countries —especially low-income countries—have seen strong and steady growth. Only 20 percent have increased their per capita income by 2.5 percent a year or more since 1980. Moreover, only 30 developing countries maintained such growth rates in five or more consecutive years. But recently developing countries have been growing faster. Between 2000 and 2005 half of all developing countries achieved growth of 2.5 percent a year or higher in per capita income.

Economic growth does not always bring immediate reduction in poverty. Even in fast-growing economies, poor people may not share equally in the benefits of growth. For a given rate of growth, the rate of poverty reduction depends on the initial level of inequality and how the distribution of income changes with growth. If inequality increases, poverty reduction will be slower. A country with high initial inequality will need to grow faster than a country with more equal income distribution to achieve the same poverty reduction. To achieve broad-based economic growth, all people must have equal opportunity to participate.

The average growth of developing countries has accelerated since 2000

Annual growth of GDP per capita (%)

Source: World Development Indicators database

Benefits of growth are not shared equally by everyone

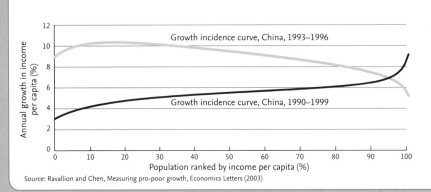

A growth incidence curve shows how fast income grew at each income level. In China, between 1990 and 1999, the incomes of the wealthiest people grew fastest.

But for a brief period, between 1993 and 1996, poor people's income grew faster (yellow line).

Source: Ravallion and Chen, Measuring pro-poor growth, Economics Letters (2003)

Thandi Farm, Elgin, South Africa, a wine, fruit and vegetable farm, is owned and run by the workers

Equality of opportunity does not mean equal outcomes. However, if all members of society have similar chances to become socially active, politically influential, and economically productive, sustainable long-run development is more likely because the allocation of resources is more efficient. When economic and social institutions systematically favor the interests of those with higher status and greater resources, the economy is likely to be less efficient, missing out on opportunities for innovation and investment.

There are many ways to increase the opportunities for poor people. First, they need access to education and health services, which increase productivity. Water and sanitation systems help to reduce the incidence of disease. Particularly in rural areas, improvements to transportation and communication systems are needed to improve access to markets. Secure tenure to property increases incentives for new investment on the part of rural and urban dwellers. Protection through the rule of law reduces risks and uncertainties that undermine growth.

There is considerable inequality of opportunity in education in some developing countries

School participation rate (%), age 6–11, by wealth quintile

■ Benin
☐ Vietnam

Source: Demographic and Health Survey, Benin 2001 and Vietnam 2001

Countries that have grown fastest have made the greatest reductions in poverty

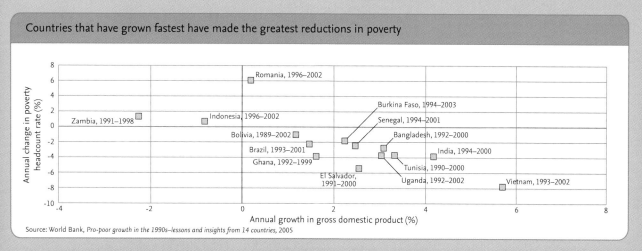

Source: World Bank, *Pro-poor growth in the 1990s–lessons and insights from 14 countries*, 2005

Economic growth

average annual growth of GDP per capita, 2000–2005

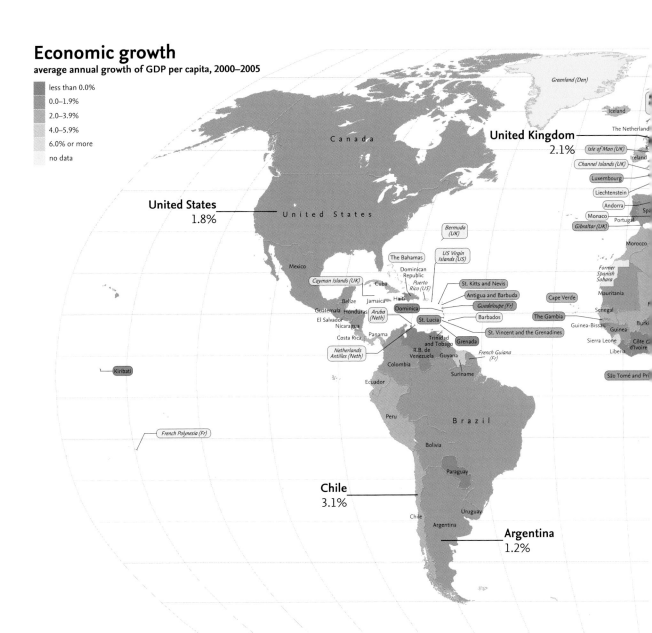

- less than 0.0%
- 0.0–1.9%
- 2.0–3.9%
- 4.0–5.9%
- 6.0% or more
- no data

United Kingdom 2.1%

United States 1.8%

Chile 3.1%

Argentina 1.2%

Map labels: Greenland (Den), Iceland, The Netherland, Canada, Isle of Man (UK), Ireland, Channel Islands (UK), Luxembourg, Liechtenstein, Andorra, Monaco, Portugal, Spain, Gibraltar (UK), Morocco, United States, Bermuda (UK), Mexico, The Bahamas, US Virgin Islands (US), Former Spanish Sahara, Dominican Republic, Puerto Rico (US), St. Kitts and Nevis, Mauritania, Cayman Islands (UK), Cuba, Antigua and Barbuda, Cape Verde, Belize, Jamaica, Haiti, Guadeloupe (Fr), Senegal, Guatemala, Honduras, Aruba (Neth), Dominica, Barbados, The Gambia, Burki, El Salvador, St. Lucia, Guinea-Bissau, Guinea, Nicaragua, St. Vincent and the Grenadines, Sierra Leone, Côte d'Ivoire, Costa Rica, Panama, Trinidad and Tobago, Grenada, Liberia, Netherlands Antilles (Neth), R.B. de Venezuela, Guyana, French Guiana (Fr), São Tomé and Prí, Colombia, Suriname, Ecuador, Kiribati, Peru, Brazil, French Polynesia (Fr), Bolivia, Paraguay, Uruguay, Chile, Argentina

China has the fastest GDP growth rate of the developing countries

Long-term growth of GDP per capita

Rank	Country	Annual growth rate 1990–2005
1	China	8.7
2	Vietnam	5.8
3	Ireland	5.1
4	Rep. of Korea	4.6
5	Chile	4.1
6	India	4.1
7	Trinidad and Tobago	4.1
8	Lebanon	4.0
9	Mozambique	3.9
10	Singapore	3.8

China
8.9%

Vietnam
6.3%

India
5.3%

Ethiopia
2.1%

Sri Lanka
3.7%

South Africa
3.2%

Facts	Internet links	
All six developing regions grew faster in 2005 than their average growth rate between 1990 and 2004.	▶ World Bank – Global Economic Prospects	**www.worldbank.org/prospects**
Nearly 60 percent of all developing economies grew faster in 2005 than their average growth rate between 1990 and 2004.		
95 percent of Europe and Central Asian economies and 75 percent of Sub-Saharan African economies grew faster in 2005 than their previous average performance.	▶ IMF World Economic Outlook	**www.imf.org/weo**
The last 15 years saw a surge of growth, especially among countries that opened their economies to trade and investment, maintained sound monetary and fiscal policies, and strengthened the rule of law.	▶ OECD statistics	**www.oecd.org/statistics**

Inequality

share of income or consumption going to the poorest quintile

1983–2004, most recent year available

- less than 3.0%
- 3.0–4.9%
- 5.0–6.9%
- 7.0–8.9%
- 9.0% or more
- no data

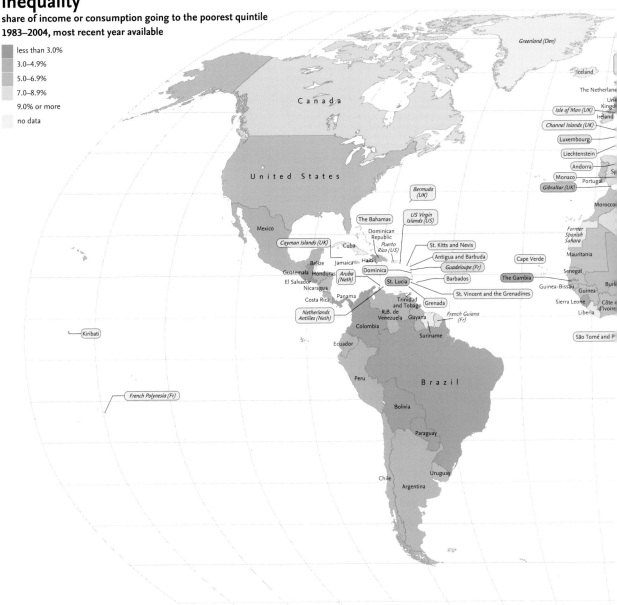

Ten countries with high inequality ratios

One commonly used measure of income inequality is the inequality ratio, calculated as the ratio of income or consumption shares of the richest 20 percent to the poorest 20 percent of the population. A ratio of 10 means that the top 20 percent of the population earns (or spends) ten times as much as the bottom 20 percent of the population. Generally the higher this ratio, the more unequal the income distribution. Countries with high inequality ratios are mostly in Latin America and Africa. The highest inequality ratio among Asian countries is 12.

Country	Year	Income or consumption shares	Inequ rat
Sierra Leone	1989	Consumption	5
Namibia	1993	Income	5
Lesotho	1995	Consumption	4
Bolivia	2002	Income	4
Central African Republic	1993	Consumption	3
Botswana	1993	Consumption	3
Paraguay	2002	Income	2
Haiti	2001	Income	2
Colombia	2003	Income	2
Panama	2002	Income	2

Facts	Internet links	
▶ Income inequality between countries increased until the onset of rapid economic growth in China and India in the past two decades.	▶ World Development Report 2006	**www.worldbank.org/wdr**
▶ Inequality within countries has increased in many parts of the world, including Bangladesh, China, Russia, the United Kingdom, and the United States.	▶ Human Development Report	**hdr.undp.org**
▶ Inequality in access to schooling has fallen as school participation rates have risen in most countries.		
▶ Different groups of citizens within an economy, defined by such characteristics as race or gender, often face quite different opportunities for economic and social mobility.	▶ World Development Indicators	**www.worldbank.org/data**

Poverty and hunger lead to malnutrition and infant mortality

Poverty—the lack of income and essential goods and services— exists everywhere, but there has been progress. The proportion of people in developing countries living in extreme poverty has fallen from 28 percent in 1990 to 19 percent in 2002. Still, more than 1 billion people live on less than $1 a day, a number that is unacceptably high.

Global poverty has been falling since the 1980s, perhaps for the first time in human history. A poverty line set at $1.08 a day (in 1993 purchasing power)—commonly called $1 a day— is often used as the working definition of extreme poverty. Based on this, the number of people living in extreme poverty fell from 1.5 billion in 1981 to 1.2 billion in 1990 and to less than 1.1 billion in 2002. This is an important success, but greater effort will be required to further reduce poverty. Many obstacles threaten to trap hundreds of millions of people in poverty, especially in South Asia and

Sub-Saharan Africa. Poor health and lack of education deprive people of productive employment; environmental resources have been depleted or spoiled; and corruption, conflict, and misgovernance waste public resources and private investment.

The significant reduction in extreme poverty over the past two decades disguises large regional differences. The greatest decline occurred in East Asia and Pacific, led by China, where the poverty rate fell from 58 percent in 1981 to 12 percent in 2002. Over the same period, the poverty rate in South Asia fell from 52 percent to 31 percent. In contrast, the poverty rate actually increased in Sub-Saharan Africa

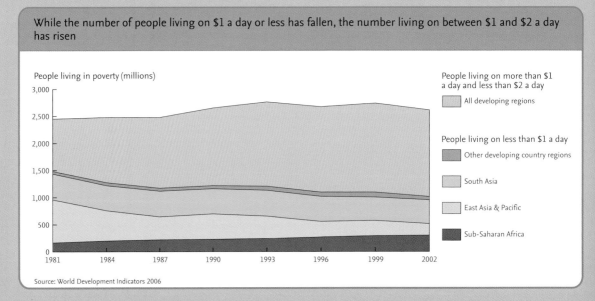

While the number of people living on $1 a day or less has fallen, the number living on between $1 and $2 a day has risen

People living in poverty (millions)

People living on more than $1 a day and less than $2 a day
- All developing regions

People living on less than $1 a day
- Other developing country regions
- South Asia
- East Asia & Pacific
- Sub-Saharan Africa

Source: World Development Indicators 2006

from 42 percent to 44 percent and the number of people living in poverty nearly doubled. The Millennium Development Goals (MDGs) call for 1990 poverty rates to be cut in half by 2015. At present many countries are falling short of that goal.

The average daily income of those living on less than $1 a day in most regions increased slightly in the 1990s. However, a marked exception is Sub-Saharan Africa where average incomes of the poor did not increase—remaining at a meager $0.62 a day—pointing to the severity and depth of poverty in this region.

Undernourishment and extreme poverty often go hand in hand. Hunger and malnutrition cause tremendous human suffering, killing millions of children every year and costing developing countries billions of dollars through lost productivity. It is estimated that 852 million people worldwide were undernourished in 2000–2002, a decrease of only 9 million over the past decade.

Sub-Saharan Africa lags in achieving the MDG target of halving the poverty rate between 1990 and 2015

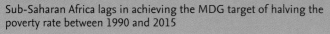

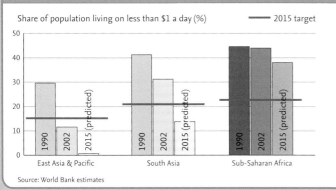

Source: World Bank estimates

Average daily incomes of the extreme poor in Sub-Saharan Africa have stagnated in the past 20 years

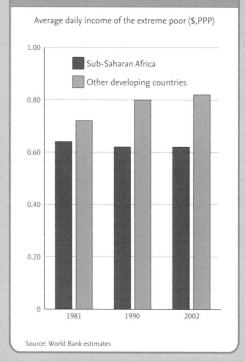

Source: World Bank estimates

53 percent of all child deaths can be attributed to being underweight

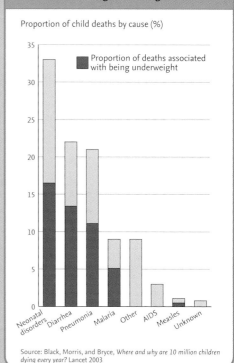

Source: Black, Morris, and Bryce, *Where and why are 10 million children dying every year?* Lancet 2003

Poverty

share of population living on less than $1 a day,
1989–2004, most recent year available

- 40.0% or more
- 20.0–39.9%
- 10.0–19.9%
- 5.0–9.9%
- less than 5.0%
- no data

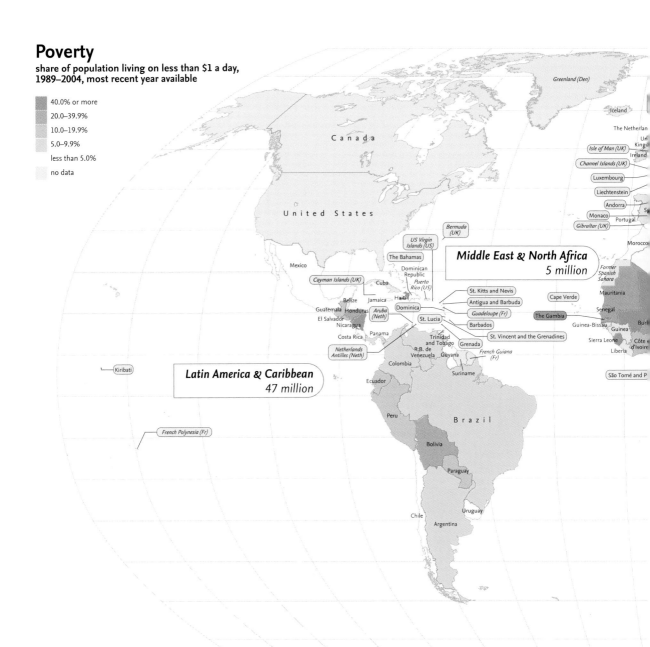

Greenland (Den)

Iceland

The Netherlan

Un
Kingd
Isle of Man (UK)
Ireland

Channel Islands (UK)

Luxembourg

Liechtenstein

Andorra

Monaco
Portugal
Gibraltar (UK)

Morocco

Canada

United States

Bermuda
(UK)

US Virgin
Islands (US)

The Bahamas

Mexico

Dominican
Republic
Puerto
Rico (US)

Cayman Islands (UK)

Cuba

Belize

Jamaica

Haiti

Guatemala Honduras   Aruba
(Neth)

Dominica

El Salvador
Nicaragua

St. Lucia

Costa Rica   Panama

Netherlands
Antilles (Neth)

Trinidad
and Tobago
R.B. de
Venezuela

Grenada

Guyana

Colombia

Suriname

Ecuador

Peru

Brazil

Bolivia

Paraguay

Chile

Uruguay

Argentina

Kiribati

French Polynesia (Fr)

Middle East & North Africa
5 million

Former
Spanish
Sahara

Mauritania

Cape Verde

Senegal

The Gambia

Guinea-Bissau   Guinea

Burk

Sierra Leone   Côte
d'Ivoire

Liberia

São Tomé and P

St. Kitts and Nevis

Antigua and Barbuda

Guadeloupe (Fr)

Barbados

St. Vincent and the Grenadines

French Guiana
(Fr)

Latin America & Caribbean
47 million

Garbage surrounds run-down buildings in rural Indonesia

People living on less than $1 a day

Country	millions (2002)
India	352
China	180
Nigeria	95
Bangladesh	43
Pakistan	26
Tanzania	20
Brazil	13
Ethiopia	12
Philippines	11
Madagascar	10

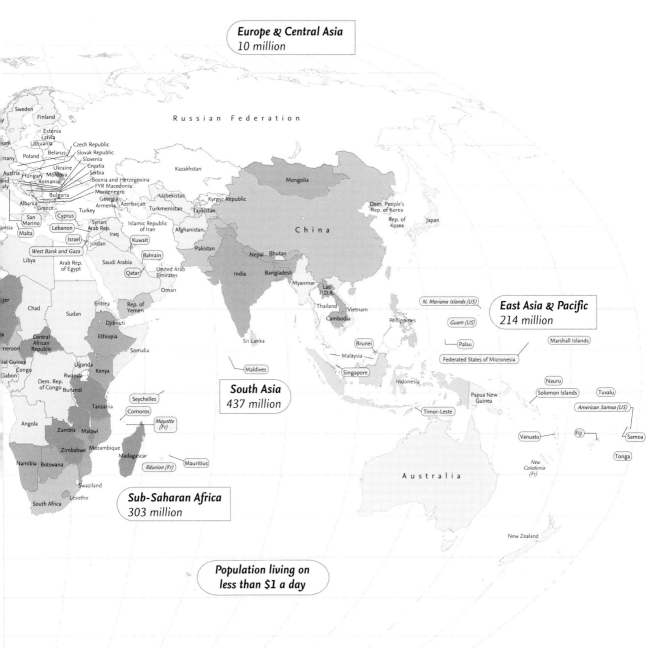

Europe & Central Asia
10 million

Russian Federation

Sweden
Finland
Estonia
Latvia
Lithuania
Czech Republic
Belarus
Slovak Republic
Poland
Slovenia
Ukraine
Croatia
Austria
Hungary Moldova
Serbia
Romania
Bosnia and Herzegovina
FYR Macedonia
Montenegro
Bulgaria
Georgia
Albania
Greece
Armenia Azerbaijan
San Marino
Cyprus
Turkey
Malta
Lebanon
Syrian Arab Rep.
Israel
West Bank and Gaza
Jordan
Libya
Arab Rep. of Egypt
Saudi Arabia
Qatar
Oman

Kazakhstan
Mongolia
Uzbekistan
Kyrgyz Republic
Turkmenistan Tajikistan
Islamic Republic of Iran
Afghanistan
Pakistan
Kuwait
Bahrain
United Arab Emirates

Dem. People's Rep. of Korea
Rep. of Korea
Japan

China

Nepal Bhutan
India Bangladesh
Myanmar
Lao P.D.R.
Thailand
Cambodia
Vietnam
Philippines

East Asia & Pacific
214 million

N. Mariana Islands (US)
Guam (US)
Palau
Marshall Islands
Federated States of Micronesia

Chad
Sudan
Eritrea
Rep. of Yemen
Djibouti
Ethiopia
Somalia
Sri Lanka
Brunei
Malaysia
Singapore
Indonesia

Central African Republic
meroon
Uganda
Rwanda Kenya
Dem. Rep. of Congo Burundi
al Guinea
Congo
Gabon
Tanzania
Seychelles
Comoros
Mayotte (Fr)

Maldives

South Asia
437 million

Nauru
Solomon Islands
Tuvalu
American Samoa (US)

Papua New Guinea
Timor-Leste

Vanuatu
Fiji
Samoa
Tonga

Angola
Zambia Malawi
Zimbabwe Mozambique
Namibia Botswana
Madagascar
Réunion (Fr)
Mauritius

Australia

New Caledonia (Fr)

Swaziland
South Africa Lesotho

Sub-Saharan Africa
303 million

New Zealand

Population living on less than $1 a day

Facts	Internet links	
Africa has more high poverty countries than any other developing country region, but Asia has the most people living in extreme poverty.	▶ World Bank: PovcalNet	**iresearch.worldbank.org/ PovcalNet/jsp/index.jsp**
Although extreme poverty occurs mostly in rural areas, urban slum populations can also have a high poverty ratio.	▶ World Bank: Country poverty estimates	**www.worldbank.org/data**
If economic growth rates in developing countries are sustained, global extreme poverty will fall to 10 percent by 2015.	▶ World Bank: Millennium Development Goals	**www.developmentgoals.org**
Many developing countries are not on track to achieve the poverty reduction target of the Millennium Development Goal of halving poverty by 2015.	▶ United Nations Millennium Project	**www.unmillenniumproject.org**

Malnourished children

proportion of children under five who are
underweight, 1995–2004, most
recent year available

- 30% or more
- 20–29%
- 10–19%
- 5–9%
- less than 5%
- no data

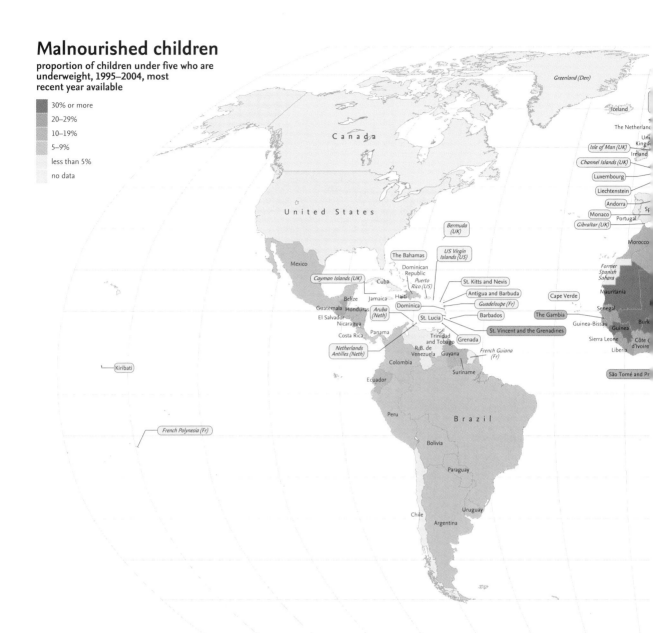

Malnourished children are vulnerable to diseases

Highest rates of malnutrition

Country	Year	children und (%)
Nepal	2001	48.3
Bangladesh	2004	47.5
Ethiopia	2000	47.2
India	1998	46.7
Timor-Leste	2003	45.8
Rep. of Yemen	2003	45.6
Cambodia	2000	45.2
Burundi	2000	45.1
Madagascar	2004	41.9
Sudan	2000	40.7

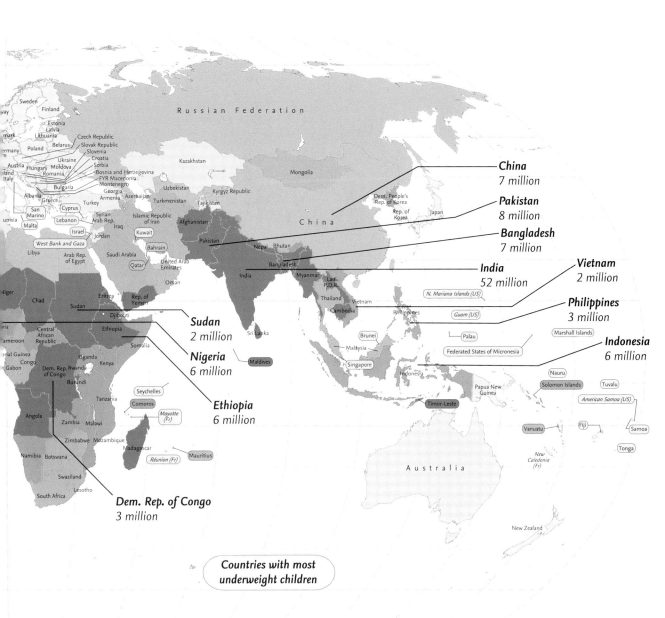

China
7 million

Pakistan
8 million

Bangladesh
7 million

India
52 million

Vietnam
2 million

Philippines
3 million

Indonesia
6 million

Sudan
2 million

Nigeria
6 million

Ethiopia
6 million

Dem. Rep. of Congo
3 million

Countries with most
underweight children

Facts	Internet links	
▸ Large disparities exist for underweight prevalence between urban and rural children and between children in rich households and poor households in the developing world.	▸ UNICEF Monitoring the Situation of Children and Women	www.childinfo.org
▸ Around 146 million children in developing countries are underweight, based on the most recent estimates.	▸ World Health Organization	www.who.int/nutgrowthdb/en
▸ Between the periods 1995–1997 and 2000–2002, the rate of increase in the number of undernourished people slowed from 5 million per year to 1 million per year in Sub-Saharan Africa.	▸ Food and Agriculture Organization	www.fao.org
▸ During the same period, the proportion of undernourished people in Sub-Saharan Africa fell from 36 percent, where it had hovered since 1990–1992, to 33 percent.	▸ World Bank	www.worldbank.org/data

The 20th century saw rapid population growth. It began with 1.6 billion, and ended with 6.1 billion living in the world. The largest increase came after 1950. The momentum created by this growth could carry the world's population beyond 7 billion by 2015, and to over 9 billion by 2050.

Crowded street, Shanghai, China

This population growth was the result of rapidly plummeting death rates, followed by more gradual declines in birth rates, first in the more developed, then, since 1950, in developing countries. Nearly all the population growth occurred in developing countries, but because of different demographic situations, there were large regional variations.

Asia, with over half the world's population in 1965, added over 1.7 billion people to its population over the next 40 years. But Sub-Saharan Africa, whose population nearly tripled in the same time period, had the highest growth rate. The populations of rich countries grew much more slowly. As a result, their share of the world population fell from 22 percent in 1965 to 16 percent in 2005.

Even as world population grew, the pace of growth decreased. Between 1965 and 1980, population grew by 1.9 percent a year; between 1980 and 2005 it grew by 1.5 percent. Every region experienced a slowdown during this period, but Sub-Saharan Africa still grew fastest, at 2.6 percent a year. By contrast, the growth rates in high-income economies and Europe and Central Asia fell sharply, to well below 1 percent a year.

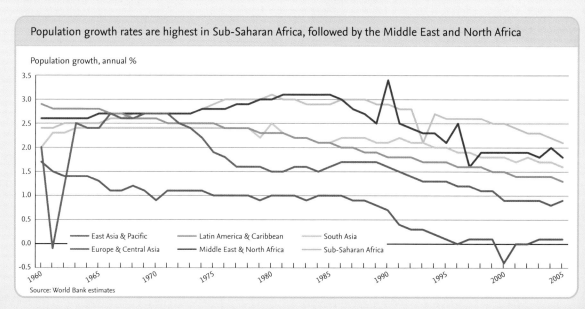

Population growth rates are highest in Sub-Saharan Africa, followed by the Middle East and North Africa

Population growth, annual %

East Asia & Pacific   Latin America & Caribbean   South Asia
Europe & Central Asia   Middle East & North Africa   Sub-Saharan Africa

Source: World Bank estimates

Patterns for absolute population increase and annual growth rates differ by regions and their demographic situations	Number (millions)			Growth rates (%)	
	1965	1980	2005	1965–1980	1980–2005
East Asia & Pacific	980.6	1,359.0	1,885.3	2.18	1.31
Europe & Central Asia	364.6	425.6	472.9	1.03	0.42
Latin America & Caribbean	247.1	357.2	551.4	2.46	1.74
Middle East & North Africa	111.4	168.2	305.4	2.74	2.39
South Asia	631.5	898.0	1,470.0	2.35	1.97
Sub-Saharan Africa	254.3	385.0	741.4	2.77	2.62
High Income	727.7	839.8	1,011.3	0.95	0.74
World	3,317.2	4,432.7	6,437.8	1.93	1.49

Source: World Bank estimates

The next billion

These trends not only shaped the current demographic profile of countries, but will influence their demographic futures. Between 2000 and 2015, an additional 1 billion people will be added to the world's population. More than half of them will be in Asia, with South Asia projected to increase by over 350 million people, and East Asia and Pacific by 230 million people. Europe and Central Asia will add a scant 3 million people. During this period, the population of Sub-Saharan Africa will continue to grow rapidly, with fertility rates remaining at over 3.5 births per woman, producing a youthful age structure. It is almost certain that the fastest population growth will be in poor countries, among the poorest population groups within these countries, and that urban areas in these regions will absorb most of the additional people. In these countries a "youth bulge" will ensure that births will continue to rise even as couples have fewer children.

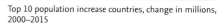
Absolute population increase by country. Most of the projected increase in the coming years will be in the poorest countries.

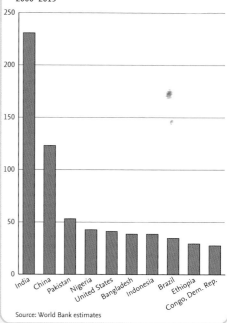
Top 10 population increase countries, change in millions, 2000–2015

Source: World Bank estimates

Many European countries will experience population decline. The largest declines will be among those countries that are currently in the midst of economic transition.

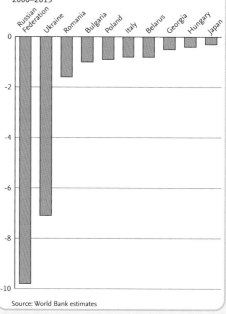
Top 10 population decrease countries, change in millions, 2000–2015

Source: World Bank estimates

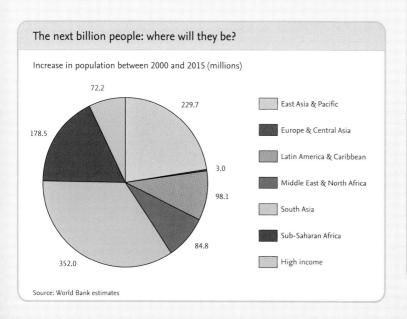
The next billion people: where will they be?

Increase in population between 2000 and 2015 (millions)

East Asia & Pacific
Europe & Central Asia
Latin America & Caribbean
Middle East & North Africa
South Asia
Sub-Saharan Africa
High income

Source: World Bank estimates

Population growth
annual average growth rate, 2000–2005

- 3.0% or more
- 2.0–2.9%
- 1.5–1.9%
- 1.0–1.4%
- less than 1.0%
- no data

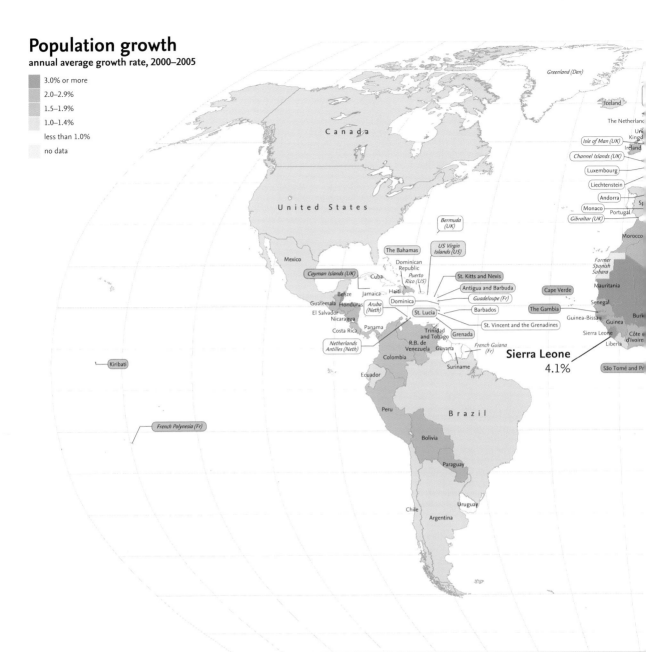

Greenland (Den)

Iceland

The Netherland

C a n a d a

Isle of Man (UK)
Uni
Kingd
Ireland

Channel Islands (UK)

Luxembourg

Liechtenstein

Andorra

Sp

U n i t e d S t a t e s

Monaco

Portugal

Gibraltar (UK)

Bermuda (UK)

Morocco

Mexico

Former
Spanish
Sahara

The Bahamas

US Virgin
Islands (US)

Dominican
Republic

Mauritania

Cayman Islands (UK)

Cuba

Puerto
Rico (US)

St. Kitts and Nevis

Cape Verde

Senegal

Belize

Jamaica

Haiti

Antigua and Barbuda

Guatemala

Honduras

Aruba
(Neth)

Dominica

Guadeloupe (Fr)

The Gambia

Guinea-Bissau

Guinea

Burk

El Salvador

Barbados

St. Lucia

Nicaragua

Costa Rica

Panama

Trinidad
and Tobago

St. Vincent and the Grenadines

Sierra Leone

Côte
d'Ivoire

Grenada

Liberia

Netherlands
Antilles (Neth)

R.B. de
Venezuela

Guyana

French Guiana
(Fr)

Sierra Leone
4.1%

Colombia

Suriname

São Tomé and Pr

Kiribati

Ecuador

Peru

B r a z i l

French Polynesia (Fr)

Bolivia

Paraguay

Chile

Uruguay

Argentina

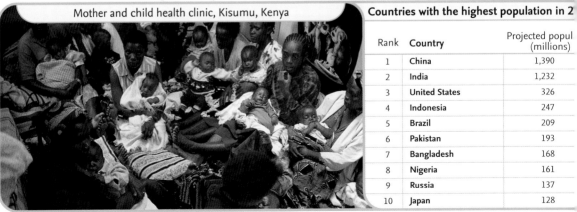

Mother and child health clinic, Kisumu, Kenya

Countries with the highest population in 2

Rank	Country	Projected population (millions)
1	China	1,390
2	India	1,232
3	United States	326
4	Indonesia	247
5	Brazil	209
6	Pakistan	193
7	Bangladesh	168
8	Nigeria	161
9	Russia	137
10	Japan	128

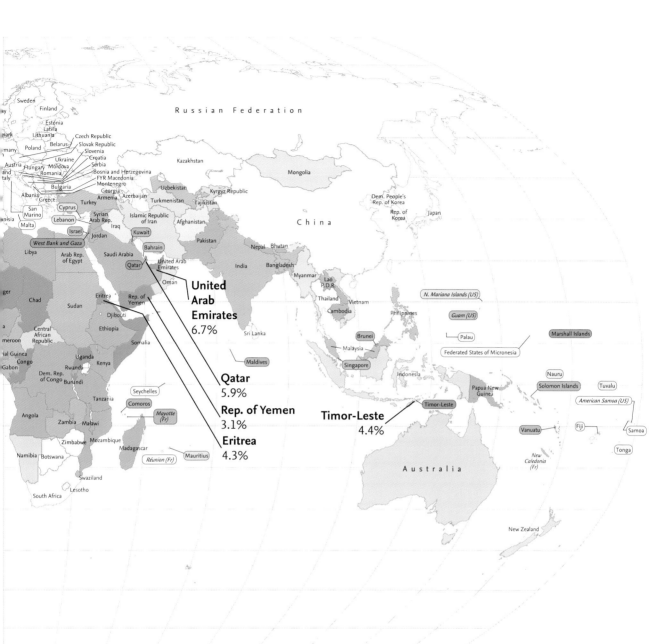

United Arab Emirates
6.7%

Qatar
5.9%

Rep. of Yemen
3.1%

Eritrea
4.3%

Timor-Leste
4.4%

Facts	Internet links	
In most countries fertility rates, rather than mortality rates, will determine future population size.	▶ UN Population Information Network	www.un.org/popin
It took human history up to the early 1800s to reach 1 billion people; today the world gains 1 billion people every 12–14 years.	▶ UN Population Fund	www.unfpa.org
	▶ Demographic and Health Surveys	www.measuredhs.com
The gap between countries with rapid and slow population growths is linked to disparities in wealth and opportunities.	▶ Population Reference Bureau	www.prb.org
Sub-Saharan Africa will experience the largest proportional increase in population, from 13 percent of the world's population today to 20 percent by 2050.	▶ World Bank	www.worldbank.org (Click on Topics then on Health, Nutrition and Population)

Demography will shape the world of our children and grandchildren. Failure to slow population growth in the poorest countries is likely to mean a lower quality of life for millions of people. The key determinants of population size and structure are fertility, mortality, and migration.

The world experienced a population explosion in the middle of the 20th century, most of it in developing countries, when two demographic trends converged—high birth rates and rapidly declining death rates. In the 1960s a preference for large families kept fertility rates high, especially in low-income countries. Children were seen as an investment—working during childhood and supporting aging parents as

Most people in developing countries are living longer

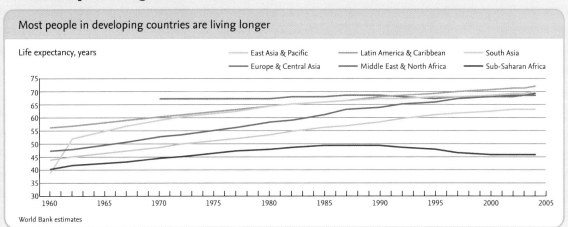

Life expectancy, years

East Asia & Pacific — Latin America & Caribbean — South Asia
Europe & Central Asia — Middle East & North Africa — Sub-Saharan Africa

World Bank estimates

A falling birth rate, but a steady death rate in high-income countries

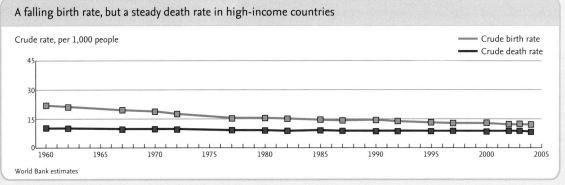

Crude rate, per 1,000 people

— Crude birth rate
— Crude death rate

World Bank estimates

Falling birth and death rates in developing countries

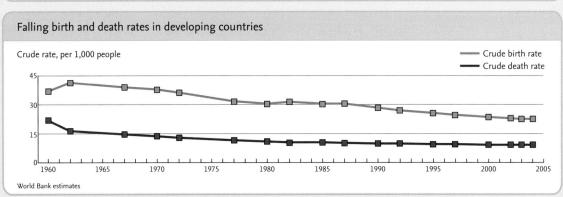

Crude rate, per 1,000 people

— Crude birth rate
— Crude death rate

World Bank estimates

adults. When mortality rates declined, so did desired family size, but in many countries, failures in health, education, and reproductive health services kept fertility rates higher for much longer.

Fertility and mortality trends have shaped the current population profiles of countries and will influence their demographic futures. In the high-income countries, increasing life expectancy has coincided with income growth and healthier lifestyles. But with a fertility rate of 1.7 births per woman, well below replacement level, the average age of the population will rise (currently 15 percent are over the age of 65) and population size may fall in the absence of immigration. In fact, large increases in migration will be needed to stabilize the labor force and maintain current levels of welfare.

In developing countries fertility rates have also declined, but at 2.8 births per woman, they remain well above those in high-income countries. The rates vary considerably by region, but remain very high in Sub-Saharan Africa. Life expectancy at birth increased steadily for the developing regions as a whole, from 41 years in 1950 to 65 years in 2004. But in Sub-Saharan Africa the HIV/AIDS epidemic has caused life expectancy to fall from 49 years to 46 years since 1990.

Decreases in life expectancy in Sub-Saharan Africa are offset by stubbornly high fertility. With over 40 percent of the population below age 15, the working-age population will bear the burden of dependent youth for some time.

Although fertility and mortality are the largest factors affecting demographic

change, migration is also important. A majority of international migrants are from developing countries. They make up a significant part of population growth in industrialized countries where fertility is so low that annual deaths exceed annual births. The departure of highly-skilled workers has affected some smaller economies but the total number of emigrants is too small to have much impact on population growth in most developing countries.

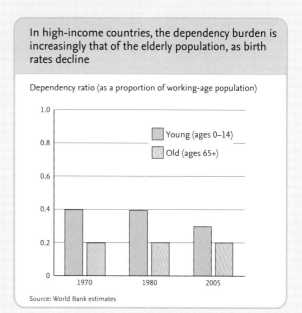

In high-income countries, the dependency burden is increasingly that of the elderly population, as birth rates decline

Dependency ratio (as a proportion of working-age population)

Source: World Bank estimates

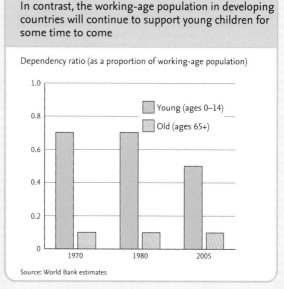

In contrast, the working-age population in developing countries will continue to support young children for some time to come

Dependency ratio (as a proportion of working-age population)

Source: World Bank estimates

Life expectancy

life expectancy at birth, 2004

- less than 55 years
- 55–64 years
- 65–69 years
- 70–74 years
- 75 years or more
- no data

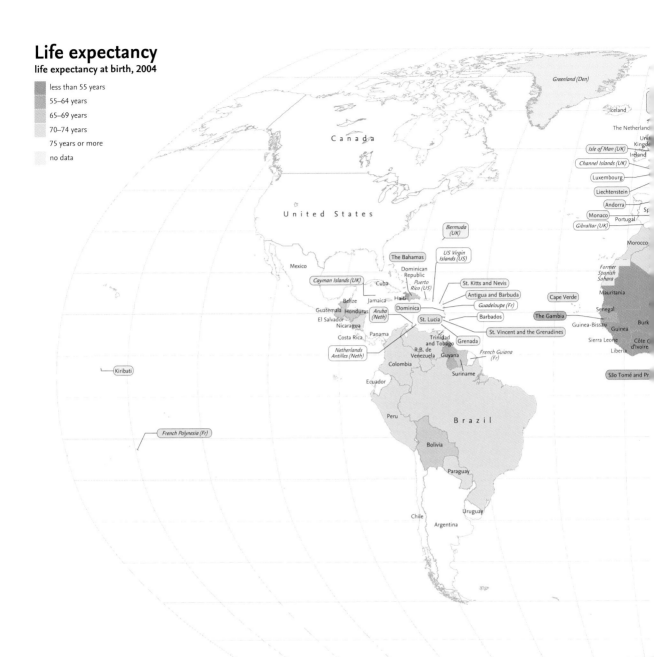

A child in Botswana can only expect to reach, on average, the age of 35

Countries with the highest and lowest life expectancies, 2

Highest countries	years
Japan	82
Switzerland	81
Sweden	81
Spain	80
Lowest countries	
Central African Republic	39
Zambia	38
Zimbabwe	37
Lesotho	36
Botswana	35

Facts	Internet links	
Over 190 million people are international migrants who live in a country other than the country of their birth.	▸ UN Population Information Network	**www.un.org/popin**
The world's population currently grows by over 200,000 people each day.	▸ UN Population Fund	**www.unfpa.org**
Population growth over the next few decades will be determined by two factors that are difficult to predict: the pace of fertility decline in some developing countries and the course of the AIDS epidemic.	▸ Demographic and Health Surveys	**www.measuredhs.com**
	▸ Population Reference Bureau	**www.prb.org**
In 11 countries population grew by three percent or more between 1990 and 2004; at this rate, a population will double in size every 23 years.	▸ The World Bank	**www.worldbank.org/data**

The movement of people across national borders is a visible and increasingly important aspect of global integration. Three percent of the world's population—more than 190 million people—are now living in countries in which they were not born. The forces driving the flow of migrants from poor countries to rich countries are likely to grow stronger in the future.

Migration is on the rise, especially from poor countries to rich countries. One reason is the large wage gap between developed and developing countries. Also increasing is the flow of remittances—currency transfers plus wages and salaries earned abroad—from migrants back to their country of origin, which has become an important source of foreign exchange for many developing countries.

Remittances have tripled since 1990, reaching almost $249 billion in 2004, with $179 billion going to developing countries. Already more than twice the size of foreign aid, remittances are expected to continue growing. Empirical studies have found that remittances can raise income levels, especially among, but not limited to, the poor. Remittances may have reduced the number of poor people in the population by 11 percent in Uganda, 6 percent in Bangladesh, and 5 percent in Ghana. In addition to benefiting households through higher levels of educational attainment, better health outcomes, and increased investment, they can also lead to improvements in the overall economy.

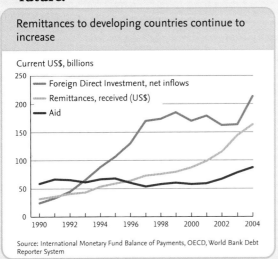

Remittances to developing countries continue to increase

Current US$, billions

Source: International Monetary Fund Balance of Payments, OECD, World Bank Debt Reporter System

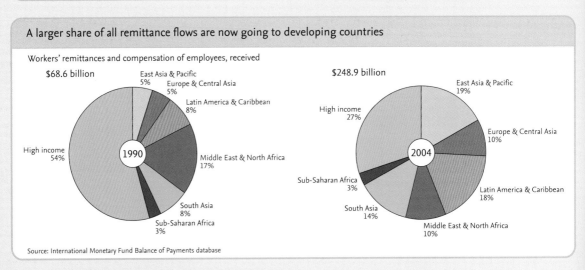

A larger share of all remittance flows are now going to developing countries

Workers' remittances and compensation of employees, received

Source: International Monetary Fund Balance of Payments database

Myanmar refugee children at their camp in Thailand

Demographic trends in both high-income and developing countries may encourage migration. In many developed countries the population is aging fast, while in many developing countries the population is young and growing rapidly. This imbalance is likely to create strong demand in high-income labor markets for developing-country workers, especially to provide services that can be supplied only locally. The share of immigrants in the total population of high-income countries increased to 11 percent in 2005, up from 7 percent two decades before.

Migration may also have negative effects. Among international migrants are millions of highly educated people who have moved to developed countries from developing countries. By migrating they improve their own prospects and provide valuable services in high-income economies, but the loss of human capital, the so-called "brain drain", from developing countries may increase the concentration of poverty and reduce the social benefits of migration. The regions most affected by the brain drain are Sub-Saharan Africa and small island economies. For example, 87 percent of Guyanese and 85 percent of Jamaicans with degrees live outside of their country.

Refugees are an important component of the migrant stock. At the end of 2005, the number of refugees stood at 8.4 million —the lowest level since 1980—accounting for 4.4 percent of the migrants in the world. In 2005, Pakistan and Iran hosted the largest number of refugees. Other major countries of asylum included Germany, Tanzania, and the United States.

Immigrants in OECD countries are better educated

Working-age immigrants by level of education, 1990 and 2000 (millions)

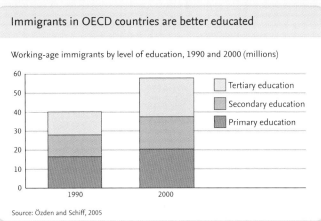

Legend:
- Tertiary education
- Secondary education
- Primary education

Source: Özden and Schiff, 2005

Immigrant populations have been growing in high-income countries since 1960 but very little in developing countries

International migration stock (total, millions)

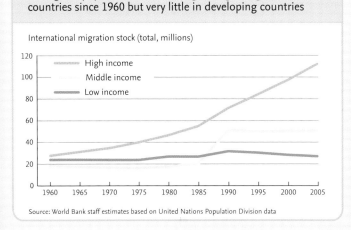

Legend:
- High income
- Middle income
- Low income

Source: World Bank staff estimates based on United Nations Population Division data

Migration
migrants as share of population, 2005

- less than 1.0%
- 1.0–2.9%
- 3.0–5.9%
- 6.0–14.9%
- 15.0% or more
- no data

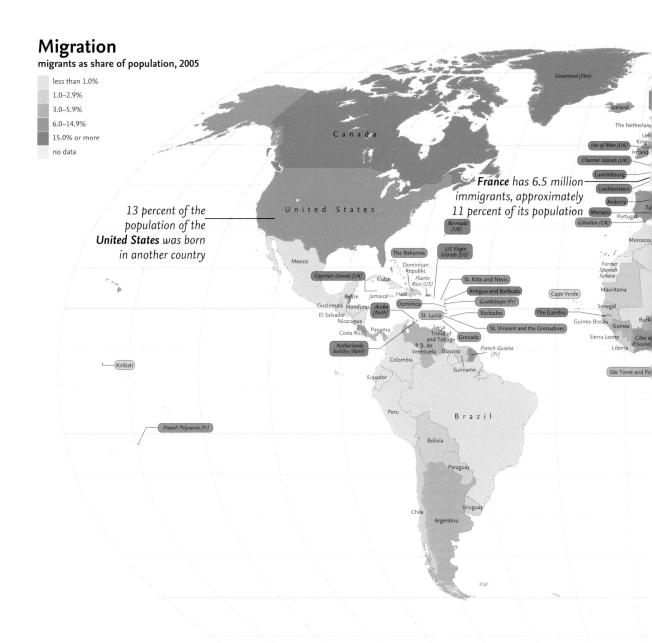

13 percent of the population of the **United States** *was born in another country*

France *has 6.5 million immigrants, approximately 11 percent of its population*

Immigrants becoming US citizens at swearing-in ceremony

Largest migrant populations, 2005

Rank	Country	millions
1	United States	38.4
2	Russian Federation*	12.1
3	Germany	10.1
4	Ukraine*	6.8
5	France	6.5
6	Saudi Arabia	6.4
7	Canada	6.1
8	India	5.7
9	United Kingdom	5.4
10	Spain	4.8

* After the breakup of the Soviet Union in 1991, people living in one of the newly independent countries who were born in another of the countries were classified as international migrants.

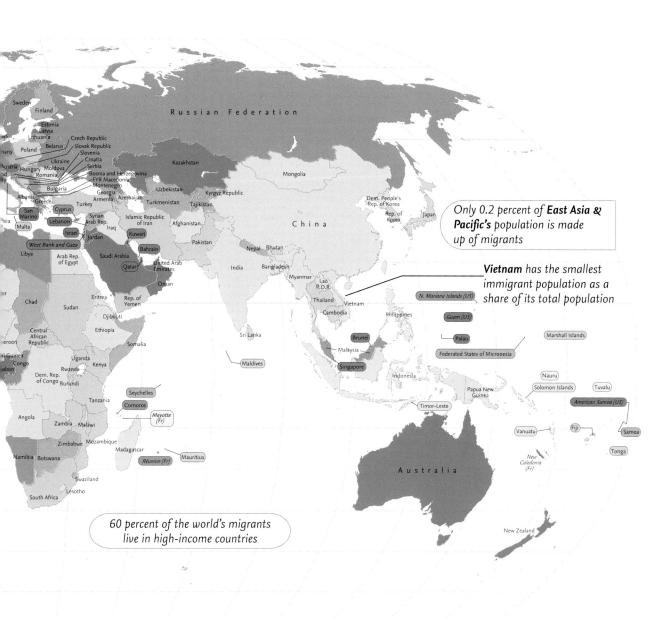

Only 0.2 percent of **East Asia &
Pacific's** population is made
up of migrants

Vietnam has the smallest
immigrant population as a
share of its total population

60 percent of the world's migrants
live in high-income countries

Facts	Internet links	
In the 1960s, the majority of migrants lived in developing countries. Today, the largest number resides in high-income countries.	▶ United Nations Population Division	**www.un.org/esa/ population/unpop.htm**
78 million migrants are living in developing countries (about 1.4 percent of their population), compared to 112 million in high-income countries (about 11 percent of their population).	▶ International Organization for Migration	**www.iom.int**
The number of migrants in the world grew from about 70 million in 1960 to more than 190 million in 2005. But this remained about 3 percent of the world's population.		
Of the immigrants in the world, 95 million are female, and 96 million are male.	▶ United Nations Refugee Agency	**www.unhcr.org**
Five countries have immigrant populations that make up more than half of their total population: Andorra, Kuwait, Monaco, Qatar, and United Arab Emirates.	▶ OECD	**www.oecd.org** Click on department, then ELS
There were 8.4 million refugees in 2005, down from 14.9 million in 1995.		

Remittances

remittances received as share of GDP, 2004

- 6.0% or more
- 3.0–5.9%
- 1.0–2.9%
- 0.5–0.9%
- less than 0.5%
- no data

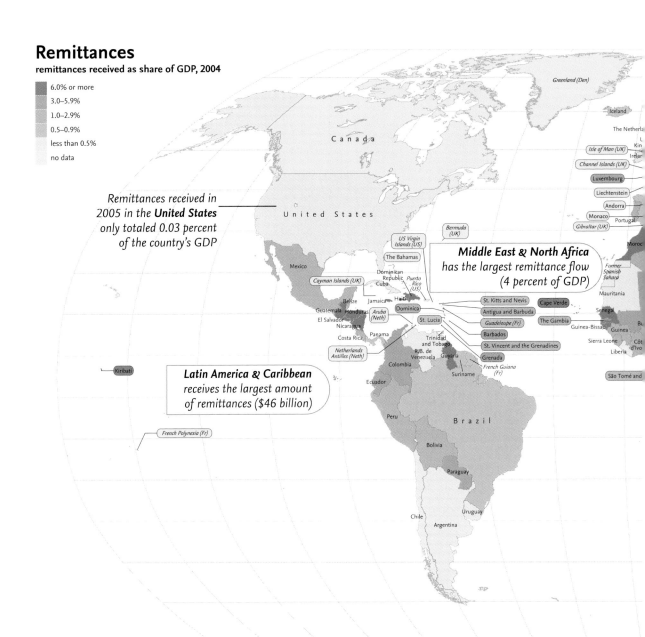

*Remittances received in 2005 in the **United States** only totaled 0.03 percent of the country's GDP*

Middle East & North Africa *has the largest remittance flow (4 percent of GDP)*

Latin America & Caribbean *receives the largest amount of remittances ($46 billion)*

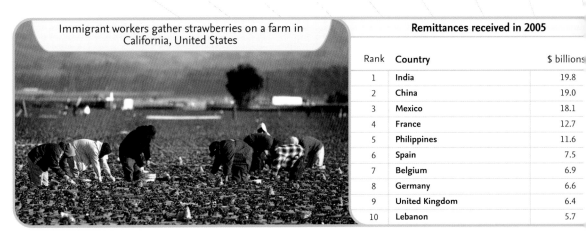

Immigrant workers gather strawberries on a farm in California, United States

Remittances received in 2005

Rank	Country	$ billions
1	India	19.8
2	China	19.0
3	Mexico	18.1
4	France	12.7
5	Philippines	11.6
6	Spain	7.5
7	Belgium	6.9
8	Germany	6.6
9	United Kingdom	6.4
10	Lebanon	5.7

Sweden
Finland
Estonia
Latvia
Lithuania
Czech Republic
Poland
Belarus
Slovak Republic
Slovenia
Croatia
Ukraine
Serbia
Austria
Hungary
Moldova
Bosnia and Herzegovina
Romania
FYR Macedonia
Bulgaria
Montenegro
Albania
Georgia
Greece
Armenia
Azerbaijan
Turkmenistan
San Marino
Cyprus
Turkey
Syrian Arab Rep.
Islamic Republic of Iran
Malta
Lebanon
Israel
Iraq
Kuwait
West Bank and Gaza
Jordan
Bahrain
Libya
Arab Rep. of Egypt
Saudi Arabia
Qatar
United Arab Emirates
Oman

Russian Federation
Kazakhstan
Mongolia
Uzbekistan
Kyrgyz Republic
Tajikistan
Afghanistan
China
Pakistan
Nepal
Bhutan
India
Bangladesh
Dem. People's Rep. of Korea
Rep. of Korea
Japan

Chad
Eritrea
Sudan
Djibouti
Rep. of Yemen
Central African Republic
Ethiopia
Somalia
Cameroon
Uganda
Eq. Guinea
Congo
Rwanda
Kenya
Gabon
Dem. Rep. of Congo
Burundi
Tanzania
Maldives
Seychelles
Comoros
Mayotte (Fr)
Angola
Zambia
Malawi
Zimbabwe
Mozambique
Namibia
Botswana
Madagascar
Réunion (Fr)
Mauritius
Swaziland
South Africa
Lesotho

Myanmar
Lao P.D.R.
Thailand
Vietnam
Cambodia
Sri Lanka
Malaysia
Brunei
Singapore
Indonesia
Philippines
N. Mariana Islands (US)
Guam (US)
Palau
Federated States of Micronesia
Marshall Islands
Nauru
Solomon Islands
Tuvalu
Papua New Guinea
Timor-Leste
American Samoa (US)
Vanuatu
Fiji
Samoa
Tonga
New Caledonia (Fr)
Australia
New Zealand

Sub-Saharan Africa
receives remittances that total only 1 percent of its GDP

At $1 million, Lao P.D.R., Malawi, the Republic of Congo, and São Tomé and Príncipe receive the smallest amounts of remittance flows

Facts

As a share of GDP, countries such as Moldova (32 percent), Tonga (31 percent), and Lebanon (26 percent) have the largest receipt of remittances. Chile (0.01 percent), Republic of Congo (0.02 percent), and Japan (0.02 percent) have the smallest.

Remittances to developing countries increased from 0.8 percent of GDP in 1990 to 1 percent in 2005. In high-income countries it remained constant at 0.2 percent.

At the beginning of the 1990s, more than half of remittances went to high-income countries. In 2005, middle-income countries received more than half of all remittances, and low-income countries received 18 percent.

In 2005, remittances were the second largest source of external financing to developing countries, after foreign direct investment, and were twice the size of aid.

High-income countries are the principal source of outward remittance flows. The United States is the largest, with $40 billion in outward flows. Saudi Arabia is the second largest, followed by Switzerland and Germany.

Internet links

▶ World Bank	**econ.worldbank.org** (search for 'remittances')
▶ International Monetary Fund	**www.imf.org**
▶ Migration Information Source	**www.migrationinformation.org**

Education prepares children to participate in their society and in the global economy. School enrollment rates are rising, but many children still do not enroll or complete primary schooling. Ensuring that all children receive a good quality education is the foundation of sustainable development and poverty alleviation.

Since 1990 the world has promised that by 2015 all children would be able to complete a full course of primary education. Primary completion rates—the proportion of each age group finishing primary school—directly measure progress towards this goal. One region, East Asia and Pacific, has already reached the target. Two other regions, Europe and Central Asia and Latin America and the Caribbean, are on track to achieve the goal. But Sub-Saharan Africa, with a primary completion rate of just 60 percent, and South Asia where completion rates average only 87 percent, are in danger of falling short.

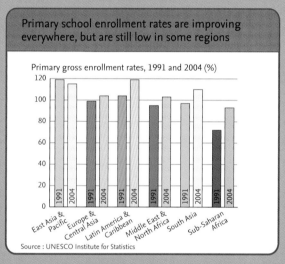

Primary school enrollment rates are improving everywhere, but are still low in some regions

Primary gross enrollment rates, 1991 and 2004 (%)

Source : UNESCO Institute for Statistics

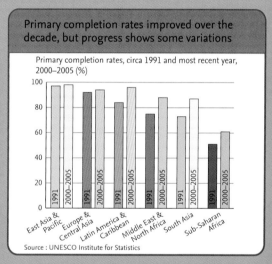

Primary completion rates improved over the decade, but progress shows some variations

Primary completion rates, circa 1991 and most recent year, 2000–2005 (%)

Source : UNESCO Institute for Statistics

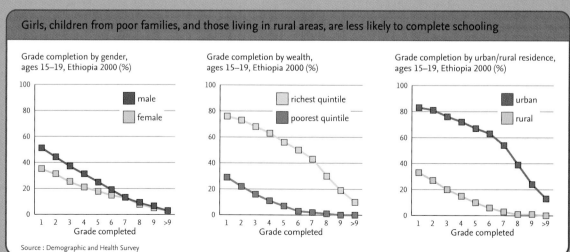

Girls, children from poor families, and those living in rural areas, are less likely to complete schooling

Grade completion by gender, ages 15–19, Ethiopia 2000 (%)

male
female

Grade completion by wealth, ages 15–19, Ethiopia 2000 (%)

richest quintile
poorest quintile

Grade completion by urban/rural residence, ages 15–19, Ethiopia 2000 (%)

urban
rural

Grade completed

Source : Demographic and Health Survey

Community school, Macaci, Abidjan, Côte d'Ivoire

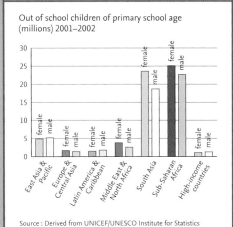

The majority of the children who are not in school are in Sub-Saharan Africa and South Asia

Out of school children of primary school age (millions) 2001–2002

Source : Derived from UNICEF/UNESCO Institute for Statistics
Children out of school: measuring exclusion from primary education

Worldwide, it is estimated that about 100 million primary school-age children still remain out of school. Three-quarters of these are in Sub-Saharan Africa and South Asia. In contrast, not more than 6 percent of the children in East Asia and Pacific and Latin America and the Caribbean are out of school .

More boys than girls are enrolled and complete primary schooling, both at the regional and country levels. Children in poor families and those living in rural areas are less likely to enroll in school and more likely to drop out earlier. There are many reasons why children drop out and stay out of school or never enroll in school: schools may be inaccessible, especially in rural areas; parents may keep children at home because of high school costs; or there may be demands for children's labor.

Beyond primary schooling

To compete in today's knowledge-driven economy and shifting global markets, countries need a flexible, skilled work force, able to create and apply knowledge. This is usually achieved through strong secondary and tertiary education systems. While all regions have made progress in expanding secondary and tertiary enrollments between 1991 and 2004, only two regions, Europe and Central Asia and Latin America and the Caribbean, have enrollment ratios above 80 percent in secondary education; and only Europe and Central Asia have tertiary enrollment ratios reaching 50 percent.

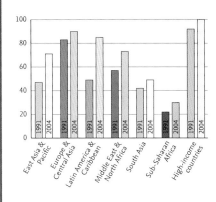

Secondary and tertiary enrollments in all regions lag behind those of developed countries

Secondary gross enrollment ratios, 1991 and 2004 (%)

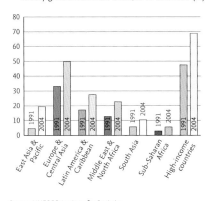

Tertiary gross enrollment ratios, 1991 and 2004 (%)

Source: UNESCO Institute for Statistics

Education for all

primary completion, 2000–2005, most recent year available

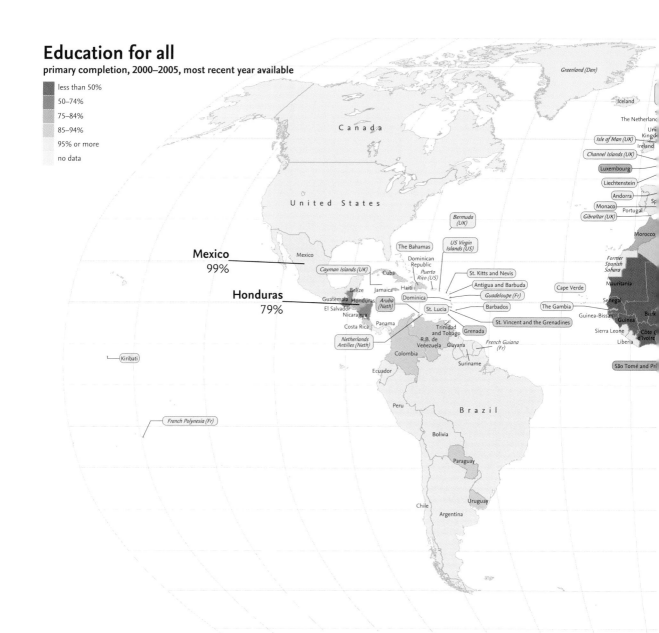

- less than 50%
- 50–74%
- 75–84%
- 85–94%
- 95% or more
- no data

Mexico 99%

Honduras 79%

In rural areas children often face a long walk to school

Lowest primary completion rates, 2000–20

Rank	Country	%
1	Niger	25
2	Guinea-Bissau	27
3	Djibouti	29
4	Burkina Faso	29
5	Chad	30
6	Mozambique	30
7	Burundi	33
8	Rwanda	37
9	Eritrea	43
10	Côte d'Ivoire	43

Facts	Internet links	
Almost one in five (18 percent) of all primary school-age children in the world are not in school.	► UNESCO Institute for Statistics	www.uis.unesco.org
Globally, 62 million girls of primary school age are not in school, accounting for 53 percent of the total number of children out of school.	► World Bank's EdStats	www.worldbank.org/ education/edstats
Women are less literate than men: worldwide, only 88 adult women are considered literate for every 100 men.	► Demographic and Health Surveys (DHS)	www.measuredhs.com
132 million of the 771 million people without literacy skills are ages 15–24 years.	► DHS data on education indicators	devdata.worldbank.org/ edstats/td16.asp
19 countries in Sub-Saharan Africa have primary completion rates of 50 percent or less.	► Organisation for Economic Co-operation and Development	www.oecd.org

The economic and social status of women has improved. More girls than ever before are enrolled in school, women's labor force participation remains steady, and fertility rates are declining. But persistent inequalities also keep women at a disadvantage and limit the ability of societies to grow, reduce poverty, and govern effectively.

Gender inequality begins at an early age and keeps women at a disadvantage throughout their lives. In 2002, 62 million girls did not attend primary school, and about two thirds of all the illiterate adults —over 500 million—are women. In some countries, girls are less likely to receive medical treatment when they are ill than boys because of parental discrimination and neglect. Mothers' illiteracy and lack of schooling directly disadvantage their young children. For example, children of mothers with no education are twice as likely to die before their fifth birthday compared to the children of mothers with secondary education.

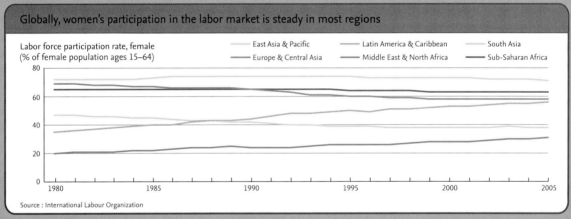

Globally, women's participation in the labor market is steady in most regions

Labor force participation rate, female (% of female population ages 15–64)

East Asia & Pacific   Latin America & Caribbean   South Asia
Europe & Central Asia   Middle East & North Africa   Sub-Saharan Africa

Source : International Labour Organization

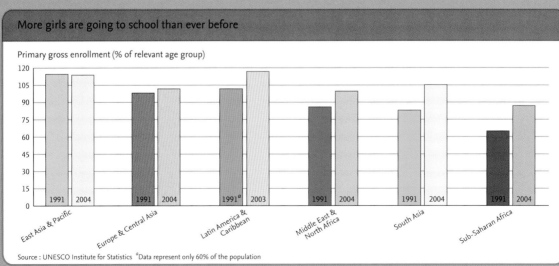

More girls are going to school than ever before

Primary gross enrollment (% of relevant age group)

East Asia & Pacific: 1991, 2004
Europe & Central Asia: 1991, 2004
Latin America & Caribbean: 1991[a], 2003
Middle East & North Africa: 1991, 2004
South Asia: 1991, 2004
Sub-Saharan Africa: 1991, 2004

Source : UNESCO Institute for Statistics [a]Data represent only 60% of the population

Women's share of employment declines as size of firm increases, Egypt, 2003		
Size of firm	Average wages Egyptian pounds, 2002	Women as % of total employment
1 worker	112.8	17.1
2–4 workers	172.1	9.4
5–9 workers	290.1	7.9
10–24 workers	1073.4	5.9
Total (firms of all sizes)	**160.1**	**14.3**

Source: UNIFEM, 2005. *Progress of the World's Women*

Persistent gender disparities in primary and secondary education, family responsibilities, and the lack of control over the timing and spacing of births, limit women's opportunities in the labor market. Women are often concentrated in more precarious and lower quality employment. Although women's participation in the labor force has increased, women are more likely to work as unpaid family workers or occupy low-paid, low-status jobs. Within any employment status, women's earnings tend to be lower than men's. A small and micro-enterprise survey for Egypt showed that while workers' wages increased with firm size, women accounted for a decreasing share of total employment. Taken together, less rewarding employment opportunities and lower wages mean that women face a higher risk of poverty.

In no region of the developing world do women have equal access to social services and productive resources, and women's participation in politics and government also remains limited, making it difficult for them to influence policy. Such disparities can have serious implications for development. A recent study estimates that a country failing to meet the Millennium Development Goal's target of providing equal access to all levels of education will suffer a deficit in per capita income growth of 0.1–0.3 percentage points.

Boys are more likely than girls to receive medical treatment

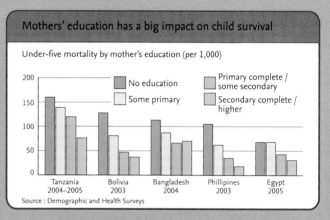

Children under 5 with acute respiratory infection taken to health provider (%)

Source : Demographic and Health Surveys

Mothers' education has a big impact on child survival

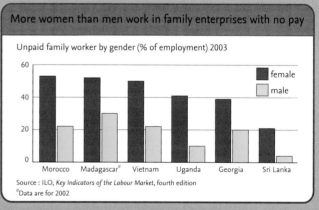

Under-five mortality by mother's education (per 1,000)

Source : Demographic and Health Surveys

More women than men work in family enterprises with no pay

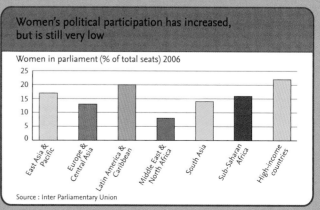

Unpaid family worker by gender (% of employment) 2003

Source : ILO, *Key Indicators of the Labour Market*, fourth edition
[a]Data are for 2002

Women's political participation has increased, but is still very low

Women in parliament (% of total seats) 2006

Source : Inter Parliamentary Union

Gender equity

ratio of girls to boys in primary and secondary
education, 2000–2005, most recent year available

- less than 90%
- 90–94%
- 95–99%
- 100–104%
- 105% or more
- no data

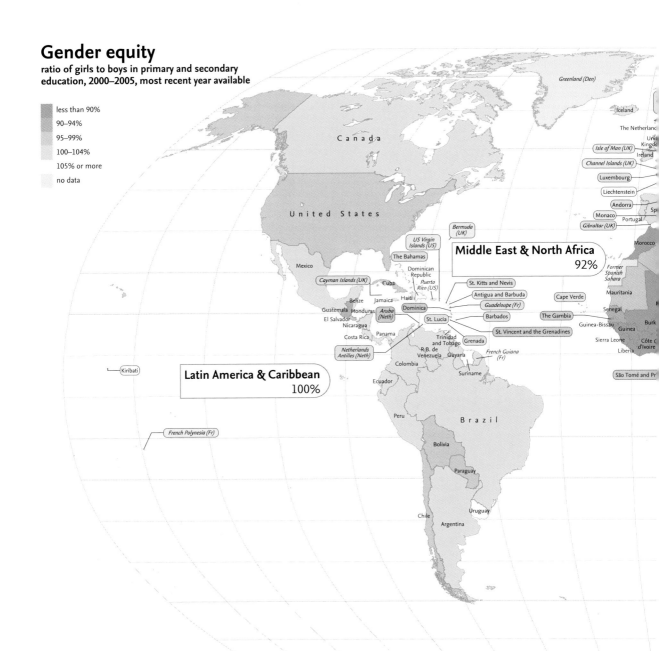

Middle East & North Africa
92%

Latin America & Caribbean
100%

Women Center, Dushanbe, Tajikistan. Women
empowerment project.

	Countries with the lowest ratios of female to male enrollment, 2000–2005	
Rank	Developing countries	Ratio (%
1	Afghanistan	41
2	Chad	58
3	Rep. of Yemen	63
4	Guinea-Bissau	65
5	Cote d'Ivoire	68
6	Niger	71
7	Eritrea	71
8	Benin	72
9	Guinea	72
10	Liberia	73

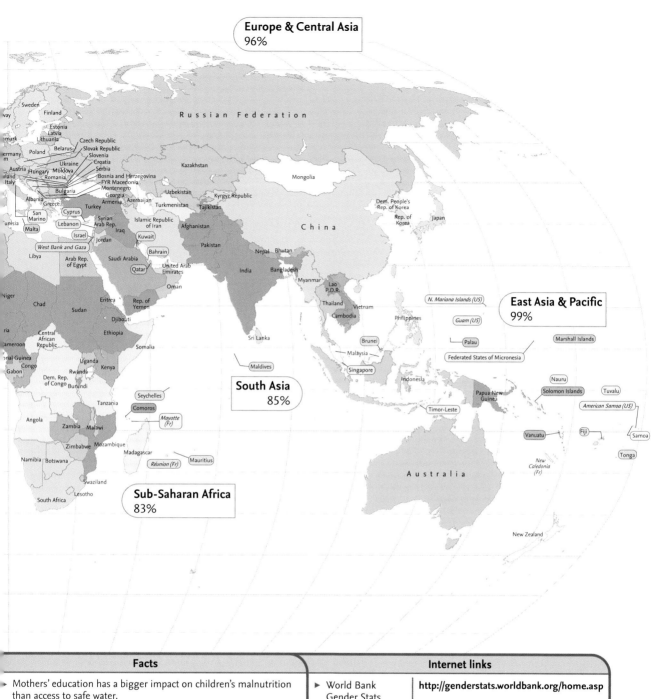

Europe & Central Asia
96%

East Asia & Pacific
99%

South Asia
85%

Sub-Saharan Africa
83%

Facts	Internet links	
► Mothers' education has a bigger impact on children's malnutrition than access to safe water.	► World Bank Gender Stats	http://genderstats.worldbank.org/home.asp
► Nearly half of the 39 million adults living with HIV are women.	► Demographic and Health Surveys	www.measuredhs.com
► Girls in both Asia and Latin America take on more child and elderly care responsibilities than boys, resulting in increased household chores and lower levels of schooling.	► UNESCO Institute for Statistics	www.uis.unesco.org
	► Inter Parliamentary Union	www.ipu.org
► In three Sub-Saharan African countries, women spend between 300 and 800 hours a year collecting fuel wood; in contrast, men spend less than 50 hours.	► International Labour Organization	www.ilo.org

Each year, more than 10 million children die before their fifth birthday, the vast majority from causes preventable through a combination of good care, nutrition, and simple medical treatment. Child mortality is thus closely linked to poverty, with child malnutrition implicated in more than half the deaths worldwide.

Child mortality has declined in every region since 1960, when 1 in 5 children died before the age of 5. By 1990, this rate had fallen to 1 in 10 children. Since then, progress has slowed, and a few countries actually experienced increases in child mortality. In 2004, 47 countries had under-five mortality rates greater than 100 per 1,000. Eleven countries—all of them in Sub-Saharan Africa—had under-five mortality rates greater than 200. In low-income countries today, 1 child in 8 dies before its fifth birthday, compared with 1 in 143 in high-income countries.

Developing countries still see many children die before the age of five

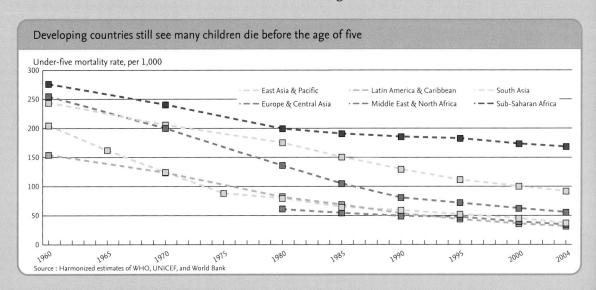

Under-five mortality rate, per 1,000

East Asia & Pacific — Latin America & Caribbean — South Asia
Europe & Central Asia — Middle East & North Africa — Sub-Saharan Africa

Source : Harmonized estimates of WHO, UNICEF, and World Bank

Without adequate immunization, children will continue to die of measles and other communicable diseases

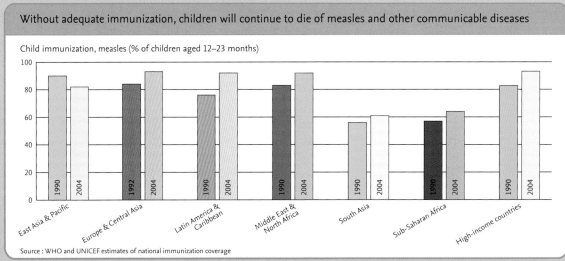

Child immunization, measles (% of children aged 12–23 months)

Source : WHO and UNICEF estimates of national immunization coverage

Children of a slum-dwelling family have a high risk of dying before the age of five

Just five diseases—pneumonia, diarrhea, malaria, measles and AIDS—account for half of all deaths in children under five. Children in Sub-Saharan Africa are hardest hit by AIDS, and in countries such as Botswana, Swaziland, and South Africa, it is estimated that child mortality more than doubled as a result of AIDS. Malnutrition is implicated in more than half of all child deaths worldwide. It weakens children and reduces their resistance to disease. It often begins at birth, when poorly nourished mothers give birth to underweight babies. Improper feeding and child care practices also contribute to worsen malnutrition.

Low-cost treatments such as antibiotics for respiratory infections, oral re-hydration for diarrhea, immunization for measles, and the use of treated bed nets in malarial regions have contributed to reducing deaths of children. In 2004, almost 75 percent of children in developing countries were immunized against measles, and deaths from measles declined by nearly two thirds in the last decade. Studies show that children from wealthier households and those living in urban areas have better access to health services and immunization, are better nourished, and so are less likely to die.

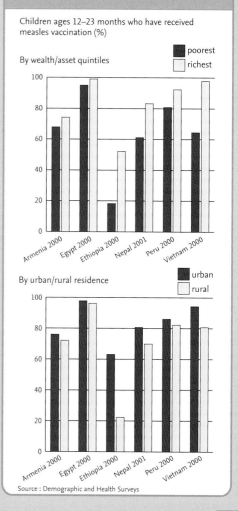

Children in Sub-Saharan Africa have been hardest hit by AIDS

Estimated impact of AIDS on under-five mortality rates, 2002–2005, selected countries in Sub-Saharan Africa

Source: UNICEF, 2005. *A call to action. Children, the missing face of AIDS*

The rich and those living in urban areas are more likely to avail themselves of health care and have better access to other services

Children ages 12–23 months who have received measles vaccination (%)

By wealth/asset quintiles

By urban/rural residence

Source : Demographic and Health Surveys

Child mortality

under-five mortality rate per 1,000, 2004

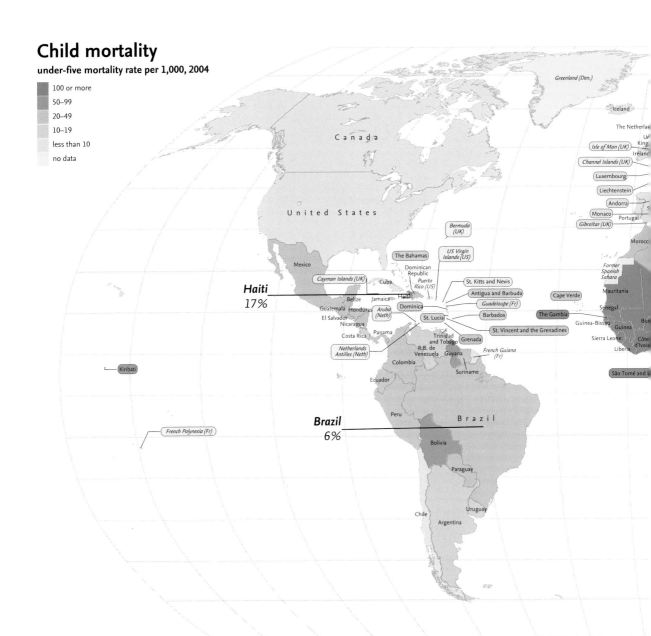

- 100 or more
- 50–99
- 20–49
- 10–19
- less than 10
- no data

Haiti
17%

Brazil
6%

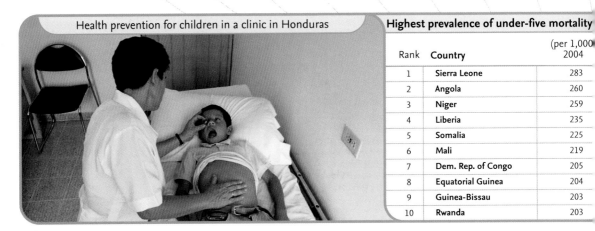

Health prevention for children in a clinic in Honduras

Highest prevalence of under-five mortality

Rank	Country	(per 1,000) 2004
1	Sierra Leone	283
2	Angola	260
3	Niger	259
4	Liberia	235
5	Somalia	225
6	Mali	219
7	Dem. Rep. of Congo	205
8	Equatorial Guinea	204
9	Guinea-Bissau	203
10	Rwanda	203

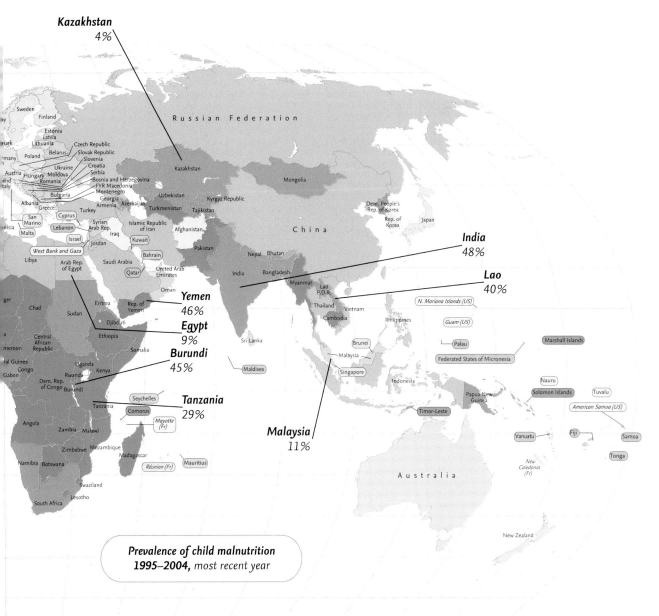

Kazakhstan
4%

Russian Federation

Kazakhstan

Mongolia

India
48%

Lao
40%

Yemen
46%

Egypt
9%

Burundi
45%

Tanzania
29%

Malaysia
11%

Prevalence of child malnutrition
1995–2004, most recent year

Australia

New Zealand

Facts	Internet links	
30,000 children a day die before their fifth birthday.	▶ UNICEF	www.childinfo.org/index2.htm
Of the 10.5 million child deaths under five every year, almost half occur in Sub-Saharan Africa.	▶ World Health Organization	www.who.int/en
Almost half the children under age five in South Asia are underweight.		
In 2020 the number of malnourished children will have fallen everywhere except in Sub-Saharan Africa, where there are likely to be more than in 1997.	▶ Demographic and Health Surveys	www.measuredhs.com

Complications from pregnancy and childbirth are a leading cause of death and disability among women of reproductive age in developing countries. Every year more than 500,000 women die during pregnancy or childbirth, and at least 10 million women suffer injuries, infection, and disabilities. A majority of deaths occur in Asia and Africa, which account for 95 percent of total deaths.

Women in high-fertility countries in Africa have a 1 in 20 lifetime risk of dying from pregnancy or childbirth, compared with women in low-fertility countries in Europe, who have a 1 in 2,000 risk of dying, and in North America, who have a 1 in 3,500 risk. And risks to women from the poorest families are still greater.

High mortality rates for mothers in many countries are the result of inadequate health care during pregnancy and delivery. Only 70 percent of pregnant women in developing countries had at least one prenatal care visit during pregnancy. The rate is even lower in South Asia, where only half of the pregnant women get prenatal care. Access to skilled care is lower still, with only 60 percent of births in developing countries being attended by skilled health staff, compared to 98 percent in high-income countries. Only about 40 percent of births are assisted in South Asia and Sub-Saharan Africa.

Compounding the risks that high fertility poses to maternal health are poorly timed and inadequately spaced births, which expose women to frequent pregnancies in short intervals. Greater access to family planning can help reduce these risks to maternal health.

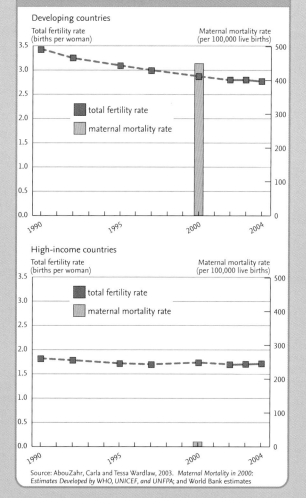

Mothers are at a much higher risk of dying during pregnancy or childbirth in developing countries

Source: AbouZahr, Carla and Tessa Wardlaw, 2003. *Maternal Mortality in 2000: Estimates Developed by WHO, UNICEF, and UNFPA*; and World Bank estimates

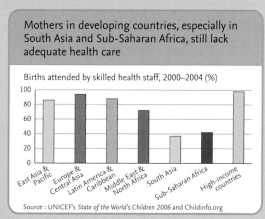

Mothers in developing countries, especially in South Asia and Sub-Saharan Africa, still lack adequate health care

Source : UNICEF's *State of the World's Children 2006* and Childinfo.org

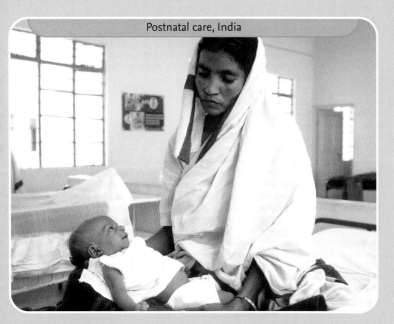
Postnatal care, India

Teenage mothers

About 15 million babies are born to young women ages 15 to 19 each year. When girls have children early, they usually cannot continue their education and so cannot join the productive workforce. The result—they have more children than women who start families later. Teenage pregnancies are high-risk for both mother and child and lead to other problems including sexually transmitted diseases, unsafe abortion, and maternal death. In some countries in Sub-Saharan Africa, more than 40 percent of teenage girls have at least one child before the age of 18. Teenage girls in developing countries have twice as many children as girls in high-income countries.

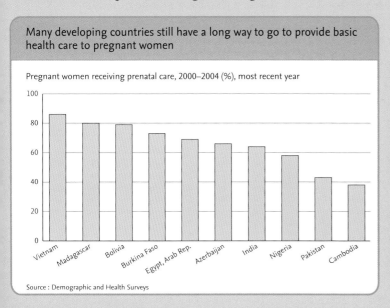

Many developing countries still have a long way to go to provide basic health care to pregnant women

Pregnant women receiving prenatal care, 2000–2004 (%), most recent year

Source : Demographic and Health Surveys

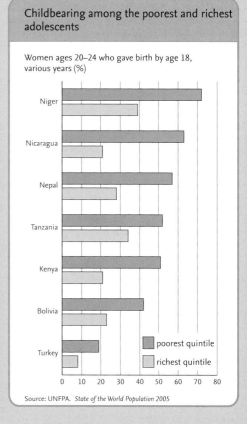

Many girls are forced into early and unsafe pregnancies by child marriage and poverty

Adolescent fertility rate, 2004
births per 1,000 women ages 15–19

Source : World Bank estimates

Childbearing among the poorest and richest adolescents

Women ages 20–24 who gave birth by age 18, various years (%)

■ poorest quintile
□ richest quintile

Source: UNFPA. *State of the World Population 2005*

Health   51

Total fertility rate

births per woman, 2004

- 4.5 or more
- 3.5–4.4
- 2.5–3.4
- 1.5–2.4
- less than 1.5
- no data

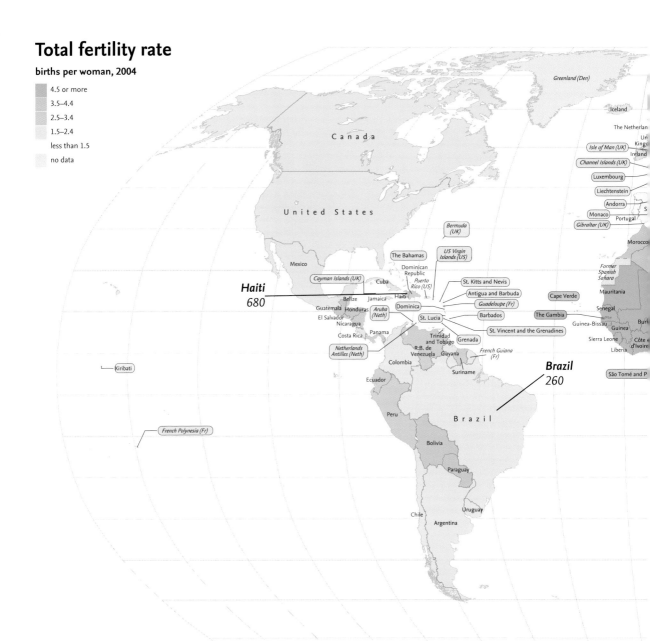

Greenland (Den)

Iceland

The Netherlan

Canada

Un
Kingo

Isle of Man (UK)

Ireland

Channel Islands (UK)

Luxembourg

Liechtenstein

United States

Andorra

Monaco Portugal

Bermuda (UK)

Gibraltar (UK)

Morocco

Mexico

The Bahamas

US Virgin Islands (US)

Former Spanish Sahara

Dominican Republic

Mauritania

Cayman Islands (UK)

Cuba

Puerto Rico (US)

St. Kitts and Nevis

Haiti
680

Haiti

Antigua and Barbuda

Cape Verde

Senegal

Belize

Jamaica

Dominica

Guadeloupe (Fr)

Guatemala

Honduras

Aruba (Neth)

St. Lucia

Barbados

The Gambia

Guinea-Bissau

Guinea

Burk

El Salvador

Nicaragua

St. Vincent and the Grenadines

Sierra Leone

Côte d'Ivoire

Costa Rica

Panama

Trinidad and Tobago

Grenada

Liberia

Netherlands Antilles (Neth)

R.B. de Venezuela

Guyana

French Guiana (Fr)

Kiribati

Colombia

Suriname

São Tomé and P

Brazil
260

Ecuador

Peru

B r a z i l

French Polynesia (Fr)

Bolivia

Paraguay

Chile

Uruguay

Argentina

A mother and child receive free vitamin A at a government health clinic, Hanoi

Countries with low levels of contraceptiv use, 2000–2004

Country	(% of wome ages 15–49
Chad	3
Sierra Leone	4
Angola	6
Guinea	7
Sudan	8
Eritrea	8
Guinea-Bissau	8
Mauritania	8
Ethiopia	8
Mali	8

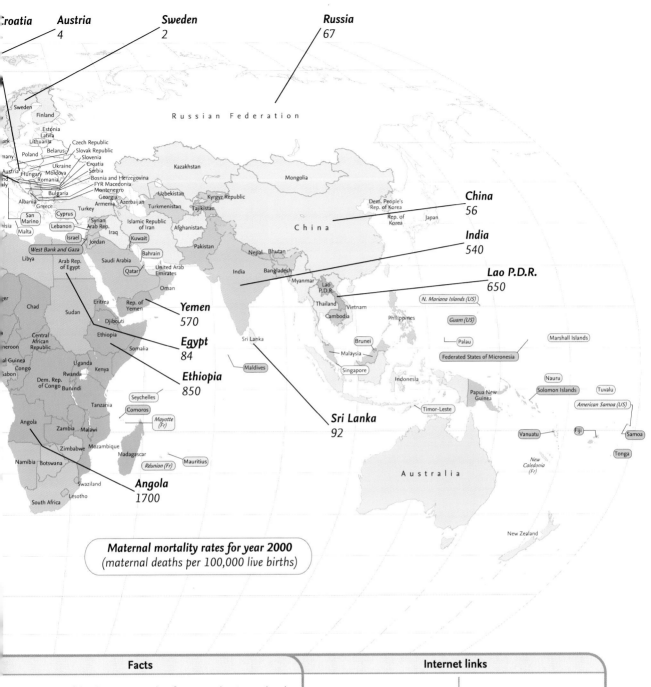

Maternal mortality rates for year 2000
(maternal deaths per 100,000 live births)

Croatia 4
Austria 4
Sweden 2
Russia 67
China 56
India 540
Lao P.D.R. 650
Yemen 570
Egypt 84
Ethiopia 850
Sri Lanka 92
Angola 1700

Facts	Internet links	
Every minute of the day, a woman dies from complications related to pregnancy or childbirth, most often in a developing country.	▶ UNICEF	www.childinfo.org/index2.htm
For every woman who dies in childbirth, 30 to 50 women suffer injury, infection, or disease.	▶ World Health Organization	www.who.int/en
Women's lifetime risk of maternal death is almost 40 times as high in the developing than the developed world.		
Severe bleeding is the leading cause of maternal deaths.	▶ Inter-agency Group on Safe Motherhood	www.safemotherhood.org

Communicable diseases take a terrible toll in developing countries. The spread of HIV/AIDS, the resurgence of tuberculosis, and increasing morbidity and mortality from malaria (mostly due to drug and insecticide resistant parasites), have had their greatest impact on poor countries and poor people, shortening life spans and curtailing economic growth.

An estimated 99 percent of all deaths from AIDS, tuberculosis, and malaria occur in developing countries. Worldwide there are 39 million people currently living with HIV/AIDS. In many countries the disease is undoing the development achievements of the past 50 years by disproportionately infecting young people and killing adults in their prime. Adolescent girls and young women are especially vulnerable to HIV and account for 60 percent of the 10 million HIV-positive youths ages 15–24. More recently, however,

A Bangladeshi health worker giving antibiotic tablets to a tuberculosis patient

countries such as Kenya and Uganda have shown a decline of HIV prevalence among young, pregnant women attending prenatal clinics.

Tuberculosis is the main cause of death from a single infectious agent among adults 15–45 years old. More than 80 percent of all tuberculosis patients live in Africa and Asia, but the epidemic is worsening in Europe and Central Asia. Poor people are especially vulnerable because of their underlying health problems and limited access to treatment.

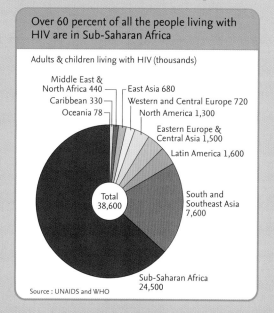

Over 60 percent of all the people living with HIV are in Sub-Saharan Africa

Adults & children living with HIV (thousands)

Middle East & North Africa 440
Caribbean 330
Oceania 78
East Asia 680
Western and Central Europe 720
North America 1,300
Eastern Europe & Central Asia 1,500
Latin America 1,600
South and Southeast Asia 7,600
Total 38,600
Sub-Saharan Africa 24,500

Source : UNAIDS and WHO

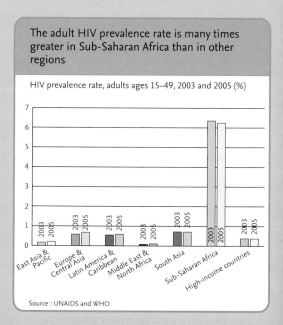

The adult HIV prevalence rate is many times greater in Sub-Saharan Africa than in other regions

HIV prevalence rate, adults ages 15–49, 2003 and 2005 (%)

East Asia & Pacific | Europe & Central Asia | Latin America & Caribbean | Middle East & North Africa | South Asia | Sub-Saharan Africa | High-income countries

2003 2005 | 2003 2005 | 2003 2005 | 2003 2005 | 2003 2005 | 2003 2005 | 2003 2005

Source : UNAIDS and WHO

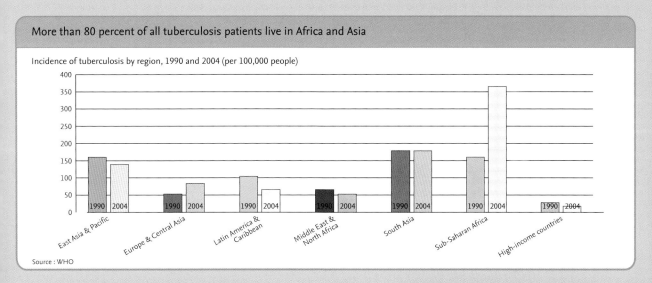

More than 80 percent of all tuberculosis patients live in Africa and Asia

Incidence of tuberculosis by region, 1990 and 2004 (per 100,000 people)

East Asia & Pacific | Europe & Central Asia | Latin America & Caribbean | Middle East & North Africa | South Asia | Sub-Saharan Africa | High-income countries

Source : WHO

And people with weak immune systems are at greater risk—in some Sub-Saharan African countries up to 60 percent of tuberculosis patients are HIV-positive.

Malaria is endemic in more than 100 countries in tropical and subtropical regions, killing more than 1 million people each year. Most deaths from malaria are among children younger than 5 years old, accounting for about 9 percent of all childhood deaths. Studies have shown that sleeping under an insecticide-treated mosquito net is an effective prevention strategy. However, the use of treated bed nets among children under five is extremely low—in Sub Saharan Africa it is only 3 percent.

Economic impact of diseases

Estimates suggest that tuberculosis can cost up to 30 percent of annual household income in lost wages.

Treated bed nets combat malaria but are not widely used

Children sleeping under treated bed nets, most recent year available, 2000–2005 (%)

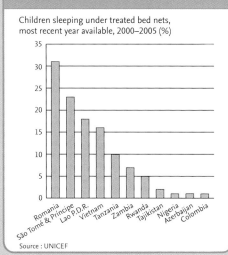

Romania | São Tomé & Príncipe | Lao P.D.R. | Vietnam | Tanzania | Zambia | Rwanda | Tajikistan | Nigeria | Azerbaijan | Colombia

Source : UNICEF

AIDS is decimating the workforce in several African countries

Workforce lost to AIDS by 2005 and 2020, selected African countries, (%)

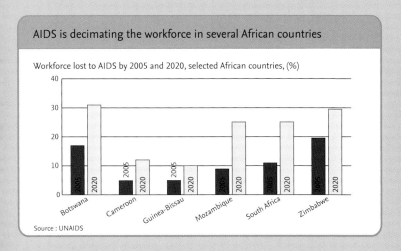

Botswana | Cameroon | Guinea-Bissau | Mozambique | South Africa | Zimbabwe

Source : UNAIDS

Malaria slows economic growth in Africa by some 1.3 percent a year. Compounded over 35 years in countries where malaria is endemic, this means that gross domestic product is about a third lower than it might have been. And when HIV/AIDS prevalence reaches 8 percent—about where it is for 11 African countries today—the cost in economic growth is estimated at about 1 percent a year.

HIV/AIDS
adult HIV prevalence, 2005

- 20.0% or more
- 10.0–19.9%
- 1.0–9.9%
- 0.5–0.9%
- less than 0.5%
- no data

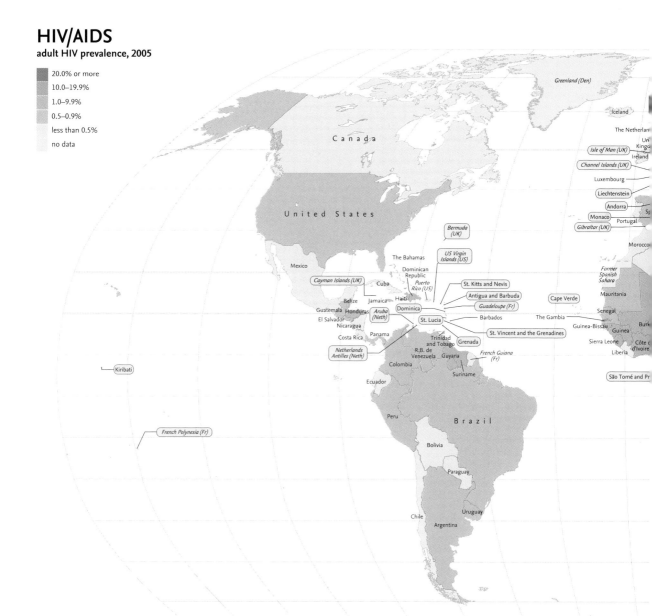

HIV/AIDS has a devastating effect on families and on the economies of the developing world

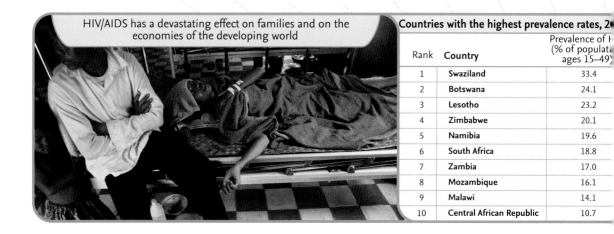

Countries with the highest prevalence rates, 2

Rank	Country	Prevalence of H (% of populat. ages 15–49)
1	Swaziland	33.4
2	Botswana	24.1
3	Lesotho	23.2
4	Zimbabwe	20.1
5	Namibia	19.6
6	South Africa	18.8
7	Zambia	17.0
8	Mozambique	16.1
9	Malawi	14.1
10	Central African Republic	10.7

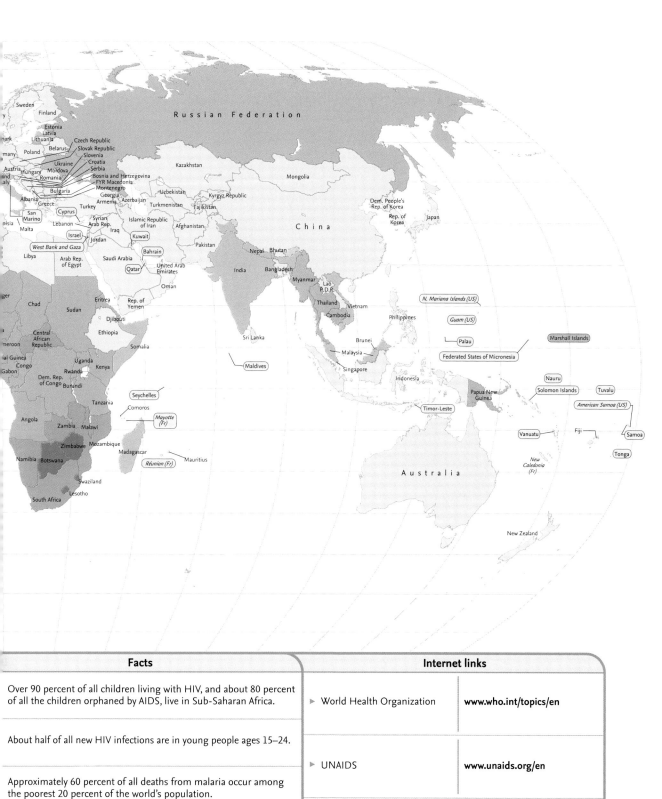

Facts	Internet links	
Over 90 percent of all children living with HIV, and about 80 percent of all the children orphaned by AIDS, live in Sub-Saharan Africa.	▶ World Health Organization	www.who.int/topics/en
About half of all new HIV infections are in young people ages 15–24.	▶ UNAIDS	www.unaids.org/en
Approximately 60 percent of all deaths from malaria occur among the poorest 20 percent of the world's population.		
95 percent of tuberculosis cases and 98 percent of deaths occur in the developing world.	▶ Demographic and Health Surveys	www.measuredhs.com

Services have been the most rapidly growing sector of the global economy and now account for almost 70 percent of world output. Developing economies are also becoming important producers of manufactured goods. However, agriculture and mining continue to be the main sources of income for many poor developing economies.

Gross domestic product (GDP) measures the output of an economy. It is the sum of value added in agriculture (including forestry and fisheries), industry (including mining and manufacturing), and services (including both government and private services). As economies develop they typically shift from a dependence on the production and export of agricultural and mining commodities to manufactured goods, and later to services. In many high-income economies more than 70 percent of GDP is produced in the service sector.

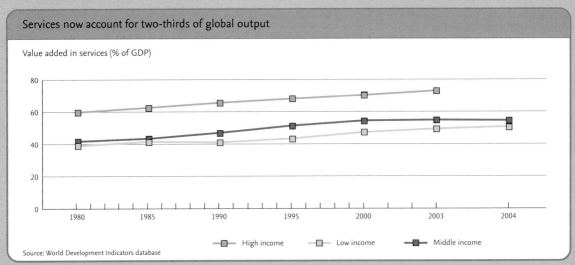

Services now account for two-thirds of global output

Value added in services (% of GDP)

Source: World Development Indicators database

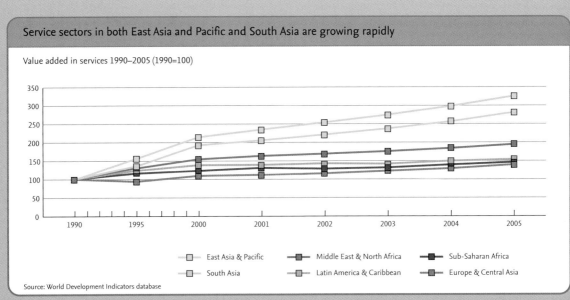

Service sectors in both East Asia and Pacific and South Asia are growing rapidly

Value added in services 1990–2005 (1990=100)

Source: World Development Indicators database

Many countries are still dependent on agricultural employment

Agricultural employment as share of total employment 2000–2003 (%)

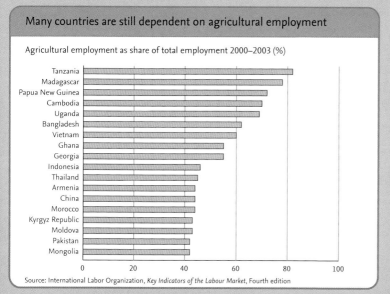

Tanzania
Madagascar
Papua New Guinea
Cambodia
Uganda
Bangladesh
Vietnam
Ghana
Georgia
Indonesia
Thailand
Armenia
China
Morocco
Kyrgyz Republic
Moldova
Pakistan
Mongolia

0   20   40   60   80   100

Source: International Labor Organization, *Key Indicators of the Labour Market*, Fourth edition

Although the service sector can contribute more than 70 percent of GDP in high-income economies...

The service sector accounts for a little more than 50 percent of the output of middle-income economies, but some, such as Jordan and Panama, have maintained large service sectors for some time. In low-income economies the service sector is growing and now accounts for slightly less than 50 percent of their output. The East Asia and Pacific region, led by China, and the South Asia region, led by India, have increased their service output nearly three-fold since 1990.

Although the service sector is growing everywhere, agriculture remains of great importance to developing economies. In 2005, value added in agriculture as a percentage of GDP was over 40 percent in eleven low-income economies, nine of them in Africa. Agriculture is also an important source of employment. It employs over 40 percent of the labor force in 18 countries, over 60 percent in seven countries, and as much as 82 percent in Tanzania. Not only low-income economies but also some middle-income economies are dependent on agriculture. Even in China, agriculture accounts for 44 percent of the total employment. In comparison, agricultural employment accounted for 4 percent of total employment in the United States and Germany, and only 1 percent in the United Kingdom and Japan.

...agriculture is still of major importance in developing countries

Agricultural output

**share of value added in agriculture in GDP,
2000–2005, most recent year available**

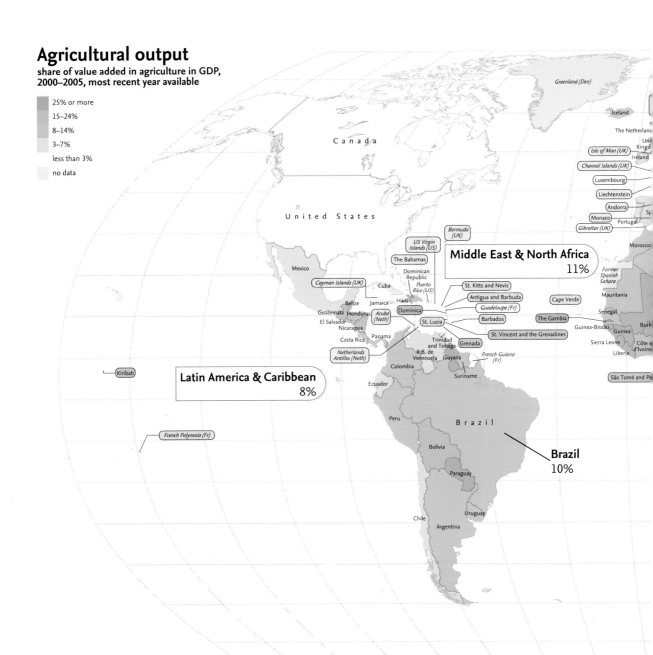

- 25% or more
- 15–24%
- 8–14%
- 3–7%
- less than 3%
- no data

Greenland (Den)

Iceland

The Netherlan

Uni
Kingd
Ireland

Isle of Man (UK)

Channel Islands (UK)

Luxembourg

Liechtenstein

Andorra

Monaco   Portugal   Sp

Gibraltar (UK)

Canada

United States

Bermuda (UK)

US Virgin Islands (US)

The Bahamas

Middle East & North Africa
11%

Morocco

Former Spanish Sahara

Mauritania

Mexico

Dominican Republic

Puerto Rico (US)

Cayman Islands (UK)

Cuba

St. Kitts and Nevis

Antigua and Barbuda

Guadeloupe (Fr)

Cape Verde

Senegal

Belize   Jamaica   Haiti

Guatemala   Honduras   Aruba (Neth)   Dominica

El Salvador

Nicaragua

St. Lucia

Barbados

The Gambia

Guinea-Bissau   Guinea

Burk

Costa Rica   Panama

St. Vincent and the Grenadines

Trinidad and Tobago   Grenada

Sierra Leone

Côte d'Ivoire

Liberia

Netherlands Antilles (Neth)

R.B. de Venezuela   Guyana

French Guiana (Fr)

Colombia

Suriname

Kiribati

Latin America & Caribbean
8%

Ecuador

São Tomé and Pi

Peru

B r a z i l

Brazil
10%

Bolivia

French Polynesia (Fr)

Paraguay

Chile

Uruguay

Argentina

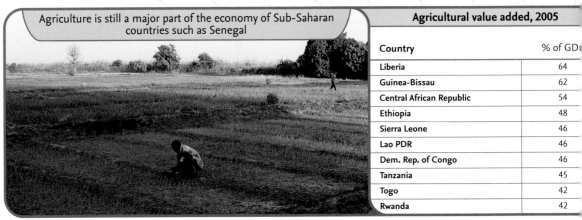

Agriculture is still a major part of the economy of Sub-Saharan countries such as Senegal

Agricultural value added, 2005	
Country	**% of GD**
Liberia	64
Guinea-Bissau	62
Central African Republic	54
Ethiopia	48
Sierra Leone	46
Lao PDR	46
Dem. Rep. of Congo	46
Tanzania	45
Togo	42
Rwanda	42

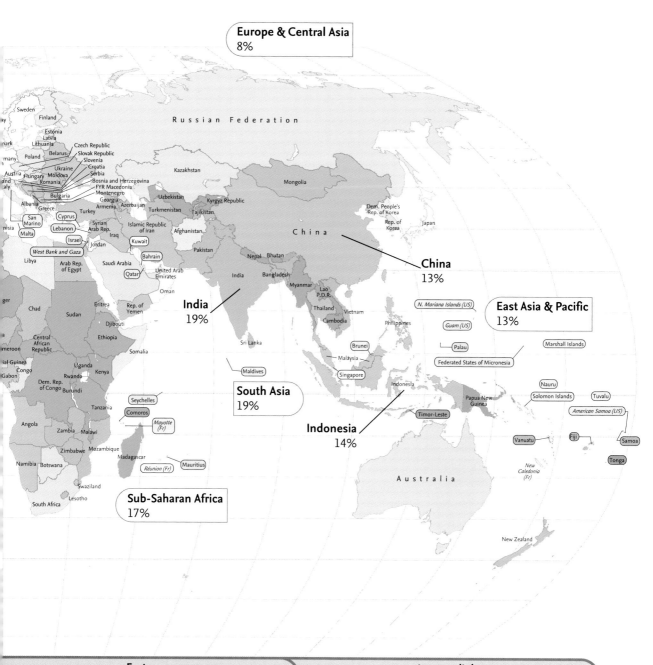

Europe & Central Asia
8%

China
13%

India
19%

East Asia & Pacific
13%

South Asia
19%

Indonesia
14%

Sub-Saharan Africa
17%

Facts	Internet links	
The world agricultural sector grew by 1.9 percent from 1990 to 2005. The service sector grew by 3.1 percent and the industrial sector by 2.3 percent over the same period.	▶ World Bank	www.worldbank.org
The highest rate of growth in agriculture from 1990 to 2005, of 3.5 percent, was registered by the Sub-Saharan African countries, where the service sector grew by 3.1 percent and the industrial sector by 2.6 percent.	▶ International Labour Organization Key Indicators of the Labour Market	www.ilo.org
In the East Asia and Pacific region, industry was the fastest growing sector with 9.7 percent growth for the period 1990 to 2005. Services were second with 7.9 percent, and agriculture grew by 3.3 percent.	▶ International Monetary Fund Data and statistics	www.imf.org
In South Asia, the fastest growing sector was services, with 7.2 percent growth, followed by 6 percent in industry, and 2.7 percent in agriculture for the same period.	▶ United Nations	www.un.org/external/data.htm

Infrastructure services—transport, energy, water and sanitation, and information and communications technology—are the backbone of a functioning economy, facilitating growth and binding communities together. Some infrastructure is built and maintained by governments; some is privately owned; and some comes about through public-private partnerships.

The services provided by infrastructure affect people in many ways—what they consume and produce; how they heat and light their homes; how they travel to work, to school, or to visit family and friends; and how they communicate. Without passable roads, farmers cannot deliver their products to markets. Without reliable electricity, manufacturers cannot compete in today's markets. And information and communications are essential in an integrated world. Infrastructure services play a key role in the most important development objective— reducing poverty and bringing real improvements in the lives of billions of people in developing countries.

Physical isolation is a strong contributor to poverty. People living in remote places have less access to health and education services, employment, and markets. Problems are particularly severe in rural areas. An estimated 900 million rural dwellers in developing countries, most of them poor, are without reliable access to affordable means of transportation. They also have less reliable electricity supplies and, in many cases, lack access to clean water and basic sanitation.

Sub-Saharan Africa has the lowest level of rural access to an all-season road among developing country regions

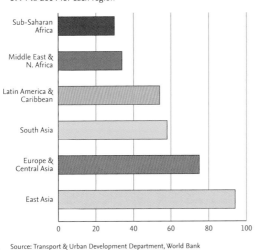

% of rural population, average of latest available data from 1994 to 2004 for each region

Source: Transport & Urban Development Department, World Bank

Water-related deaths and diseases can be sharply reduced with improvements in drinking water, sanitation, and good hygiene

▶ Improved water supply reduces diarrhea morbidity by 25 percent if severe outcomes (such as cholera) are included

▶ Improved sanitation reduces diarrhea morbidity by 32 percent

▶ Hygiene interventions including hygiene education and promotion of hand washing leads to a reduction of diarrheal cases by 45 percent

Source: WHO/UNICEF Joint Monitoring Programme for Water Supply and Sanitation, 2005. *Water for Life: Making it Happen*

Private sector participation is greatest in telecommunications

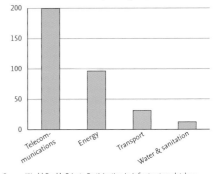

Public and private investment in developing countries in which the private sector has the operating risk, 2000–2004, $ billions

Source: World Bank's Private Participation in Infrastructure database

Women collecting water from pump in Mozambique

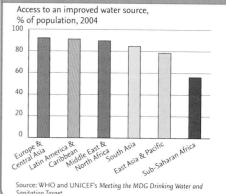
Improved water sources include water from household connections, public standpipe, borehole, a protected well or spring, or rainwater collection

Access to an improved water source, % of population, 2004

Source: WHO and UNICEF's *Meeting the MDG Drinking Water and Sanitation Target*

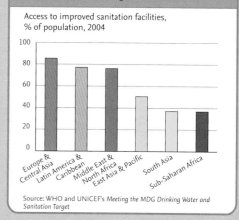
Improved sanitation facilities range from simple but protected pit latrines to flush toilets with a sewerage connection

Access to improved sanitation facilities, % of population, 2004

Source: WHO and UNICEF's *Meeting the MDG Drinking Water and Sanitation Target*

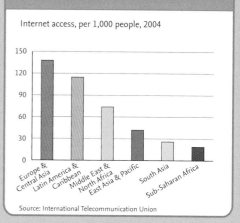
Among developing country regions, Internet access is highest in Europe and Central Asia

Internet access, per 1,000 people, 2004

Source: International Telecommunication Union

Lack of clean water and basic sanitation is the main reason that waterborne bacterial infections such as cholera are so common in developing countries. More than 2.5 billion people in the world lack safe water and sanitation services. This results in about 2 million deaths per year and hundreds of millions of cases of intestinal infection, which contribute significantly to malnutrition, mostly among children. Despite global efforts, improvements in water and sanitation infrastructure have barely kept pace with population increase and migration in the developing world. The challenge in reducing disease transmission is not only in providing better water and sanitation facilities, but also in promoting good hygiene practices, such as hand washing.

Information and communication technology has vast potential for fostering growth in developing countries. Mobile phones keep families and communities in contact and provide market information for farmers and business people. The Internet delivers information to schools and hospitals, and computers improve public and private services and increase productivity and participation.

The global supply of infrastructure services is not able to meet the needs of today, and the challenge of tomorrow, with another 2 billion people in the next 25 years, will be even greater. To meet this challenge, investment in infrastructure will need to be environmentally friendly, socially acceptable, and make a difference in improving people's lives.

Telephones

fixed-line and mobile phone subscribers per 1,000 people,
2004 or latest available data

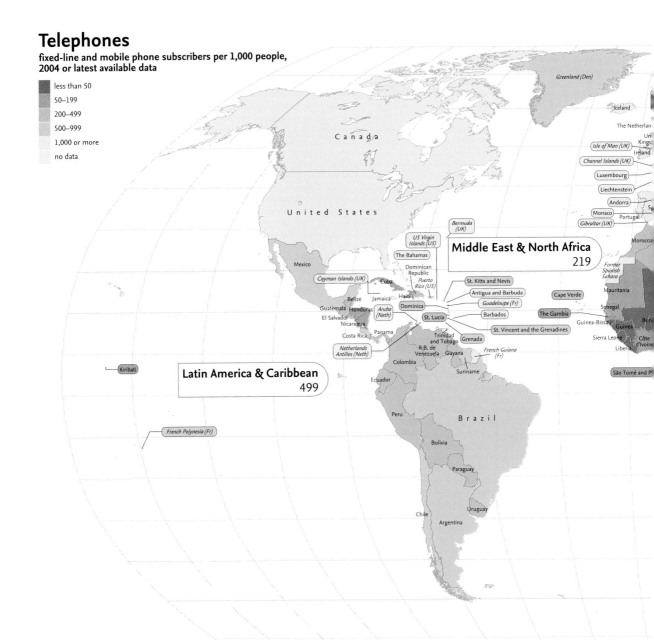

- less than 50
- 50–199
- 200–499
- 500–999
- 1,000 or more
- no data

Greenland (Den)

Iceland

The Netherlan

Un
Kingo

Isle of Man (UK)
Ireland

Channel Islands (UK)

Luxembourg

Liechtenstein

Andorra

Monaco
Portugal
Gibraltar (UK)

Canada

United States

Bermuda (UK)

US Virgin Islands (US)

The Bahamas

Mexico

Dominican Republic
Puerto Rico (US)

Middle East & North Africa
219

Morocco

Former
Spanish
Sahara

Mauritania

Cayman Islands (UK)
Cuba

Jamaica
Haiti

Belize

St. Kitts and Nevis

Antigua and Barbuda

Guadeloupe (Fr)

Cape Verde

Senegal

Guatemala
Honduras
Aruba (Neth)

Dominica

El Salvador
Nicaragua

St. Lucia

Barbados

The Gambia

Guinea-Bissau

Guinea

St. Vincent and the Grenadines

Costa Rica
Panama

Grenada

Sierra Leone

Côte
d'Ivoire

Liberia

Trinidad
and Tobago
R.B. de
Venezuela
Guyana

French Guiana (Fr)

Netherlands Antilles (Neth)

Colombia

Suriname

São Tomé and P

Kiribati

Latin America & Caribbean
499

Ecuador

Peru

Brazil

French Polynesia (Fr)

Bolivia

Paraguay

Chile

Uruguay

Argentina

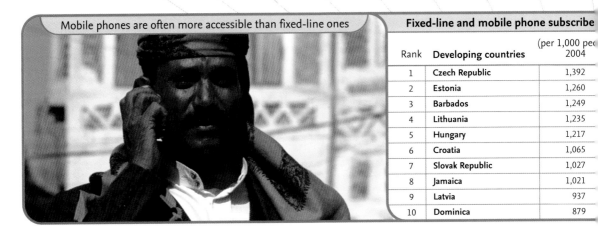

Mobile phones are often more accessible than fixed-line ones

Fixed-line and mobile phone subscribe

Rank	Developing countries	(per 1,000 peo 2004
1	Czech Republic	1,392
2	Estonia	1,260
3	Barbados	1,249
4	Lithuania	1,235
5	Hungary	1,217
6	Croatia	1,065
7	Slovak Republic	1,027
8	Jamaica	1,021
9	Latvia	937
10	Dominica	879

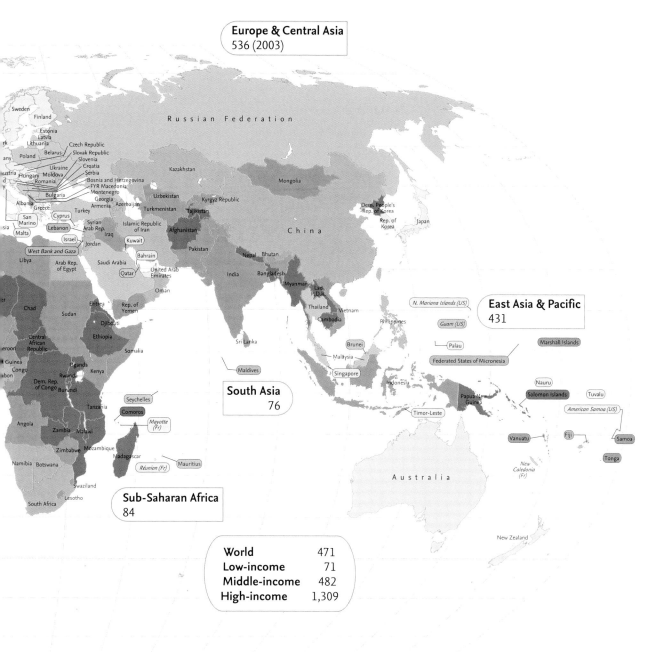

Europe & Central Asia
536 (2003)

East Asia & Pacific
431

South Asia
76

Sub-Saharan Africa
84

World	471
Low-income	71
Middle-income	482
High-income	1,309

Facts	Internet links	
Access to telephone networks (fixed-line and mobile) increased more than 10-fold between 1990 and 2004.	▶ International Telecommunication Union	www.itu.int
In 2004, all developing country regions had greater access to mobile phones than fixed-line phones.	▶ International Road Federation	www.irfnet.org
1.6 billion people lack access to modern energy services.	▶ World Resources Institute Earth Trends	earthtrends.wri.org (click on Energy and Resources)
In Sub-Saharan Africa, four times as many people have access to mobile phones than to fixed-line phones.	▶ World Bank	www.worldbank.org (click on Topics, then Information and Communication Technologies)
Among developing countries, Europe and Central Asia has the highest percentage of paved roads (74 percent), followed by the Middle East and North Africa (66 percent), South Asia (54 percent), East Asia and Pacific (32 percent), Latin America and the Caribbean (27 percent), and Sub-Saharan Africa (13 percent).	▶ Organisation for Economic Co-operation and Development	www.oecd.org (click on By Topic, then Information and Communications Technologies)
	▶ World Health Organization	www.who.int/water-sanitation-health

Investment is needed to replenish assets used up in production and increase the total capital stock. Without investment there would not be sustainable economic growth. On average, 21 percent of the world output is invested for production purposes. In East Asia and Pacific investment averages 34 percent of its output. But high rates of investment alone do not ensure rapid economic growth.

Physical investment takes many forms — buildings, machinery and equipment, improvements to property, and additions to inventories. Investment is financed out of savings, or output which is not consumed or exported. Countries that have high savings and investment rates are likely to have high rates of economic growth. Growth is also spurred by improved efficiency as a result of technological advances and investments in people, through better education and health care.

The East Asia and Pacific region has the highest investment rate among all regions, averaging 34 percent of gross domestic product (GDP). South Asia invests 28 percent of its output. Sub-Saharan Africa has the lowest investment rate, at 19.8 percent of GDP, but its rate has been increasing since 2001.

The level of investment in the East Asia and Pacific region was slightly below that of the Latin America and the Caribbean region in 1990, but now it invests more than twice as much. Similarly, South Asia and Middle East and North Africa had about the same level of investment in 1990, but now South Asia invests 37 percent more than the Middle East and North Africa region.

Investment need not be financed by domestic savings alone. Foreign direct investment through loans and equity investment has been an important source of funding for many low- and middle-income economies. Along with financial resources, foreign direct investment often brings with it access to new technologies and management skills. But to attract foreign direct investment, countries need to create a favorable investment climate. Countries that

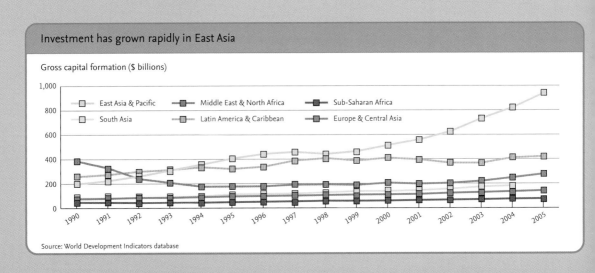

Investment has grown rapidly in East Asia

Gross capital formation ($ billions)

East Asia & Pacific · Middle East & North Africa · Sub-Saharan Africa · South Asia · Latin America & Caribbean · Europe & Central Asia

Source: World Development Indicators database

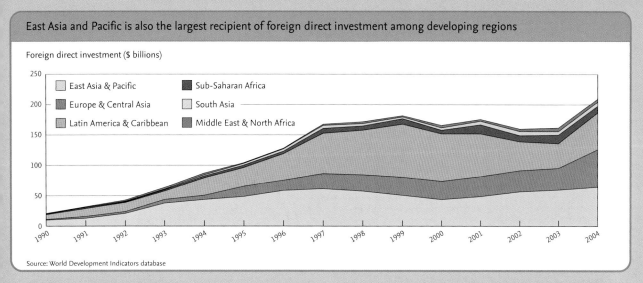

East Asia and Pacific is also the largest recipient of foreign direct investment among developing regions

Foreign direct investment ($ billions)

- East Asia & Pacific
- Europe & Central Asia
- Latin America & Caribbean
- Sub-Saharan Africa
- South Asia
- Middle East & North Africa

Source: World Development Indicators database

have neither a high savings rate nor the ability to attract foreign direct investment find themselves with limited opportunities for growth.

In 2004, $625 billion was invested abroad, with nearly two-thirds or $413 billion going to high-income economies. Developing economies received $211 billion as foreign direct investment in 2004, and their share has been climbing steadily. Between 1990 and 2004, foreign direct investment in the developing countries increased tenfold, from $21 billion to $211 billion (in current dollars).

Among the developing regions East Asia and Pacific has been the beneficiary of large amounts of foreign direct investment since the 1990s. The Latin America and the Caribbean region was the largest recipient between 1997 and 2000. But Europe and Central Asia is growing in importance, doubling its share between 2003 and 2004, and climbing to second place in 2004.

Although China and some of the other "tigers" in the East Asia and Pacific region have obtained spectacular growth rates, high levels of investment do not guarantee high growth rates. Investment produces growth, but investment also chases growth. More investment is likely in places where high returns are possible. Over the period 1990

through 1999 most developing regions invested an average of 20 to 25 percent of their GDP each year. The results obtained have varied, from Latin America and the Caribbean, where an investment ratio of 21 percent produced growth of only 2.2 percent to South Asia where an investment ratio of a little more than 22 percent resulted in annual growth of 5.8 percent. Sub-Saharan Africa is an interesting exception: a low investment ratio of 17.9 percent led to an annual growth rate of 3.7 percent, better than several regions with higher investment ratios. To produce growth, capital investment must be matched by a supportive investment climate, including an educated work force, efficient infrastructure, and efficient markets.

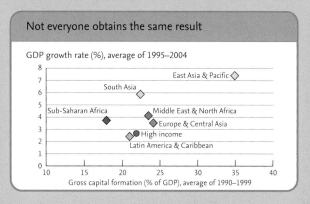

Not everyone obtains the same result

GDP growth rate (%), average of 1995–2004

East Asia & Pacific
South Asia
Sub-Saharan Africa
Middle East & North Africa
Europe & Central Asia
High income
Latin America & Caribbean

Gross capital formation (% of GDP), average of 1990–1999

Investment for growth

gross capital formation as share of GDP,
2005 or latest available data

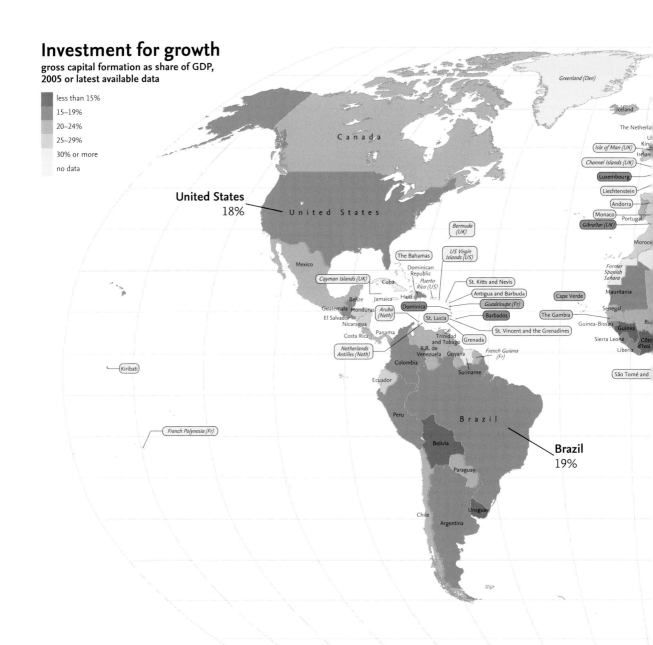

Legend:
- less than 15%
- 15–19%
- 20–24%
- 25–29%
- 30% or more
- no data

United States
18%

Brazil
19%

Map labels: Greenland (Den), Iceland, The Netherla..., Isle of Man (UK), Channel Islands (UK), Luxembourg, Liechtenstein, Andorra, Monaco, Portugal, Gibraltar (UK), Moroc..., United King..., Irela..., Canada, United States, Mexico, Bermuda (UK), US Virgin Islands (US), The Bahamas, Dominican Republic, Cayman Islands (UK), Cuba, Puerto Rico (US), St. Kitts and Nevis, Antigua and Barbuda, Guadeloupe (Fr), Cape Verde, Mauritania, Former Spanish Sahara, Jamaica, Haiti, Dominica, St. Lucia, Barbados, The Gambia, Senegal, Belize, Guatemala, Honduras, Aruba (Neth), St. Vincent and the Grenadines, Guinea-Bissau, Guinea, El Salvador, Nicaragua, Trinidad and Tobago, Grenada, Sierra Leone, Côte d'Ivoi..., Costa Rica, Panama, Netherlands Antilles (Neth), R.B. de Venezuela, Guyana, French Guiana (Fr), Liberia, Colombia, Suriname, São Tomé and..., Kiribati, Ecuador, Peru, Brazil, Bolivia, French Polynesia (Fr), Paraguay, Chile, Uruguay, Argentina

China's rapidly growing economy has benefited from foreign investment

Highest average gross capital formation

Rank	Countries greater than 1 million in population	% of GI 1995–20...
1	Lesotho	46.8
2	China	36.1
3	Turkmenistan	35.9
4	Mongolia	34.4
5	Azerbaijan	32.9
6	Korea, Rep.	31.6
7	Iran, Islamic Rep.	30.9
8	Honduras	30.6
9	Vietnam	30.5
10	Malaysia	29.7

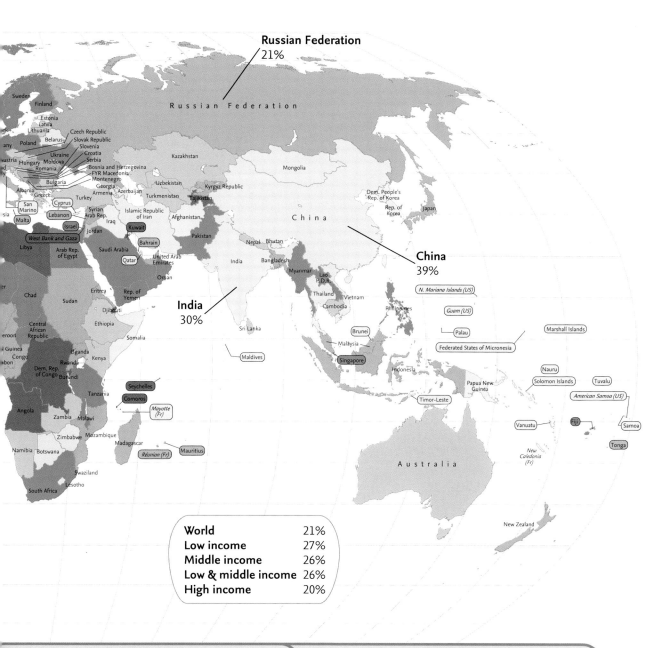

Russian Federation
21%

Russian Federation

China
39%

India
30%

World	21%
Low income	27%
Middle income	26%
Low & middle income	26%
High income	20%

Facts	Internet links	
Capital formation has been the fastest in the East Asia and Pacific region. Between 2000 and 2005 it increased at an average rate of 13 percent a year.	► World Bank – Data and Statistics	**www.worldbank.org/data**
Capital formation has been the slowest in the Latin America and the Caribbean region, growing at less than 1 percent a year between 2000 and 2005.	► Organisation for Economic Co-operation and Development	**www.oecd.org** (click on Statistics)
About 30 countries saw their investment levels decline between 2000 and 2005.	► United Nations Conference on Trade and Development	**www.unctad.org/statistics**
Investment grew at an average 48 percent a year between 2000 and 2005 in Azerbaijan.	► International Monetary Fund – Statistics	**www.imf.org/external/data.htm**
In China investment grew at an average of 15 percent a year between 2000 and 2005.		

A good investment climate is one in which government policies encourage firms and entrepreneurs to invest productively, create jobs, and contribute to growth and poverty reduction. The goal is to create an investment climate that benefits society as a whole.

The quality of the investment climate contributes strongly to growth, productivity, and employment creation—all of which are essential for sustainable reductions in income poverty.

Government policies and behaviors play a key role in shaping the investment climate. They influence the security of property rights, approaches to regulation and taxation, the provision of infrastructure, the functioning of financial and labor markets, and broader governance features such as corruption. Improving government policies and behaviors that shape the investment climate drives growth and reduces poverty.

In the past several years, the World Bank and other multilateral development banks have increased collection of data on the investment climate through the Enterprise Surveys and Doing Business surveys. Together, these survey programs help countries to identify major bottlenecks to private sector growth and to concentrate reforms to improve the business environment.

In Enterprise Surveys senior managers ranked policy uncertainty as the main business constraint, but every country is different. For example, in Bangladesh, the top business constraint is lack of reliable electricity, whereas in Hungary the main business constraint reported is high tax rates. In Guatemala, the main problem is crime, theft, and disorder.

These surveys tell us that, compared with other developing country regions, Sub-Saharan Africa is a high-cost, high-risk place to do business, resulting in less investment, less employment, lower incomes, less

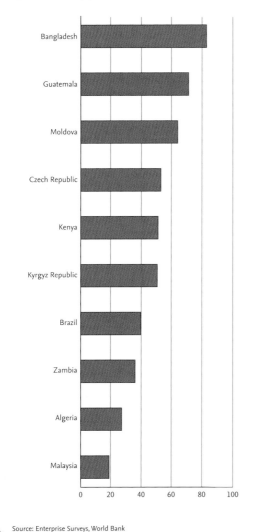

Firms in many developing countries lack confidence in the courts to uphold property rights

Managers who lack confidence in the courts to uphold property rights, 2000–2005 (%)

Source: Enterprise Surveys, World Bank

Methane gas plant, Rwanda—one of the countries that has benefited from business reforms

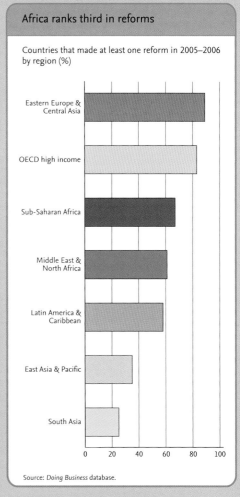

Africa ranks third in reforms

Countries that made at least one reform in 2005–2006 by region (%)

Source: *Doing Business* database.

growth and competitiveness, and higher poverty. But data for 2005–2006 also show that the pace of reform in Sub-Saharan Africa has accelerated, moving the region from last to third place in reforms.

Countries differ significantly in how they regulate the entry of new businesses. According to the most recent Doing Business survey only two countries made it more difficult to start a business in 2006. During the same time, 43 countries introduced reforms to make it easier start a business. Some countries, like Rwanda, are finding that reforms in the business environment are paying off. Beginning in 2001, Rwanda introduced new company and labor laws, followed by land titling reforms in 2002. It streamlined customs procedures, improved credit registries, and simplified judicial procedures. Since initiating reform, Rwanda has had economic growth averaging 3.6 percent a year—among the highest for non-oil-producing states in Africa.

Several countries have cut the red tape involved in starting a business between 2005 and 2006

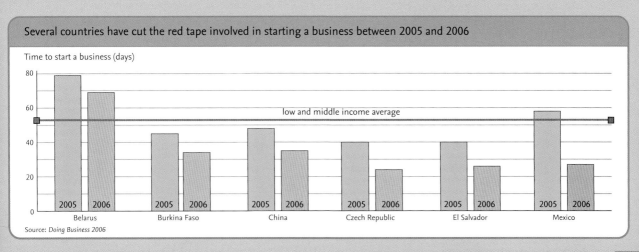

Source: *Doing Business 2006*

Starting a business

time required to start a new business, April 2006

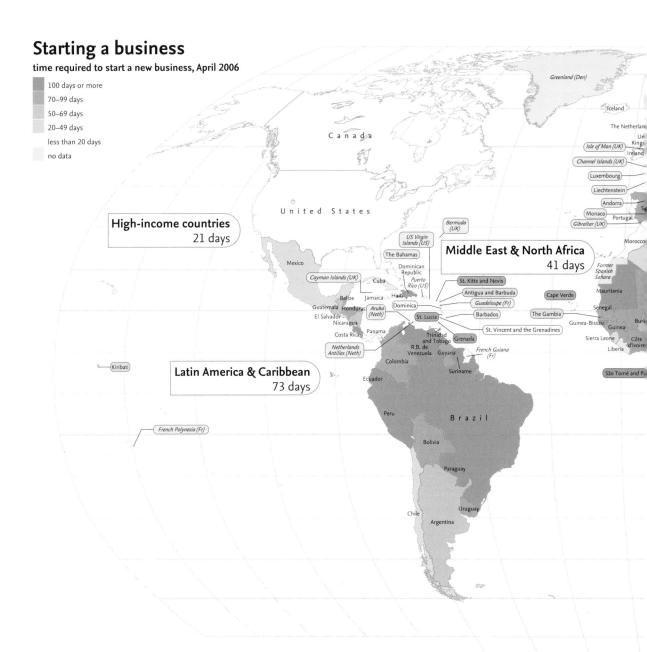

Legend:
- 100 days or more
- 70–99 days
- 50–69 days
- 20–49 days
- less than 20 days
- no data

High-income countries
21 days

Middle East & North Africa
41 days

Latin America & Caribbean
73 days

Map labels: Greenland (Den), Iceland, The Netherlands, Isle of Man (UK), United Kingdom, Ireland, Channel Islands (UK), Luxembourg, Liechtenstein, Andorra, Monaco, Portugal, Gibraltar (UK), Spain, Morocco, Former Spanish Sahara, Mauritania, Senegal, Cape Verde, The Gambia, Guinea-Bissau, Guinea, Sierra Leone, Liberia, Côte d'Ivoire, Burkina, São Tomé and Pr, Canada, United States, Mexico, Bermuda (UK), US Virgin Islands (US), The Bahamas, Cayman Islands (UK), Cuba, Dominican Republic, Puerto Rico (US), Haiti, Jamaica, Belize, Guatemala, Honduras, El Salvador, Nicaragua, Costa Rica, Panama, Aruba (Neth), St. Kitts and Nevis, Antigua and Barbuda, Guadeloupe (Fr), Dominica, St. Lucia, Barbados, St. Vincent and the Grenadines, Grenada, Trinidad and Tobago, Netherlands Antilles (Neth), R.B. de Venezuela, Colombia, Guyana, Suriname, French Guiana (Fr), Ecuador, Peru, Brazil, Bolivia, Paraguay, Chile, Uruguay, Argentina, Kiribati, French Polynesia (Fr)

Business meeting, Mozambique

Best performers—starting a business in developing countries		
Rank	Country	(days) 20
1	Afghanistan	8
2	Jamaica	8
3	Turkey	9
4	Romania	11
5	Tunisia	11
6	Morocco	12
7	St. Vincent and the Grenadines	12
8	Maldives	13
9	Central African Republic	14
10	Ethiopia, Georgia, Latvia, Micronesia, Rwanda	16

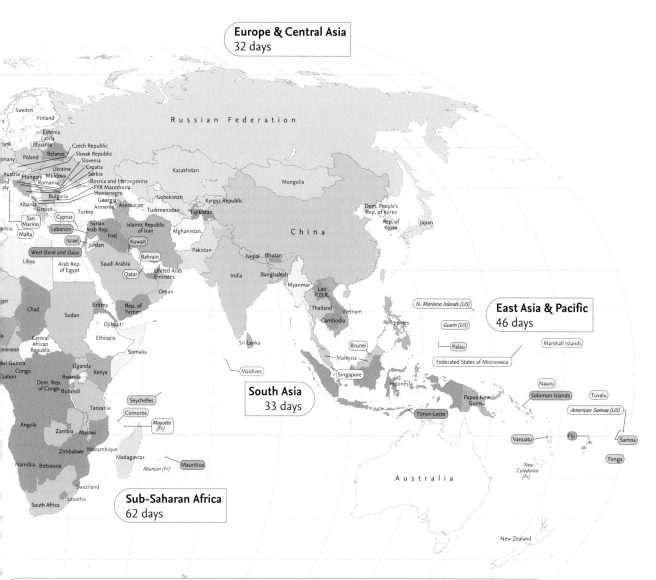

Europe & Central Asia
32 days

East Asia & Pacific
46 days

South Asia
33 days

Sub-Saharan Africa
62 days

In Canada, it takes only three days to start a business and requires two procedures.
In Republic of Korea there are 12 procedures needed to start a business, a process that takes 22 days to complete.
In El Salvador, business start-up time now takes 14 fewer days than in 2004.
Suriname's business start-up time is the highest—694 days to complete the required procedures.

Facts	Internet links	
Between 2004 and 2006, Afghanistan cut the number of procedures necessary to start a business from 28 to 3, and the time to complete the process from 90 days to 8 days.	▶ Doing Business Project World Bank	**www.doingbusiness.org**
El Salvador slashed the time required to register a business from 115 days in 2003 to 40 days in 2005 and to 26 days in 2006.	▶ Enterprise Surveys World Bank	**rru.worldbank.org/ EnterpriseSurveys/**
Two hundred and thirteen reforms in 112 economies were introduced between January 2005 and April 2006.		
Between 2003 and 2006, high-income countries cut the time needed to start a business from 31 days to 21 days, and developing countries reduced the time from 60 days to 54 days.	▶ Private Participation in Infrastructure Database	**ppi.worldbank.org**
If it is easy to set up a business, more businesses are set up—business investment increases and new jobs are created.		
Countries that introduce standardized business application forms save their entrepreneurs time, and fewer applications are rejected for flawed or insufficient paperwork.	▶ Privatization database	**rru.worldbank.org/Privatization**

Governance describes the way states acquire and exercise authority, and how they provide and manage public goods and services, including the delivery of basic services, infrastructure, and a sound investment climate. Good governance is associated with citizen participation, and overall improved accountability of public officials by citizens. It is fundamental to development and economic growth.

Governance has several dimensions: the process by which governments are selected, monitored, and replaced; the capacity of government to effectively formulate and implement sound policies; and the respect of citizens and the state for the institutions that govern interactions between them. Features of good governance such as free and fair elections, respect for individual liberties and property rights, a free and vibrant press, open and impartial judiciary, and well-informed and effective legislative structures, all contribute to strong and capable institutions of the state.

Corruption—the abuse of public office for private gain—is only one aspect of weak governance. Others include poor bureaucratic capability and ineffective checks and balances. Corruption negatively affects the provision of social services. Public sector programs such as education, health, water and sanitation are undermined when public funds earmarked for their provision are diverted for private use. This contributes to low enrollment and graduation rates and poor health outcomes. Corruption may increase the cost of doing business: firms

Control of corruption varies even within the same region

Control of corruption in South Asia, percentile ranking 2005

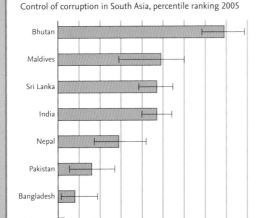

The percentile rank indicates the percentage of countries worldwide that rate below the selected country (subject to a margin of error). Higher values indicate better governance ratings. The statistically likely range of the governance indicator is shown as a thin black line. For instance, a bar extending to 75 percent with thin black lines showing a range of 60 to 85 percent means that an estimated 75 percent of countries rate worse and an estimated 25 percent rate better than that country. At the 90 percent confidence level, only 60 percent of countries rate worse, while 15 percent of countries rate better

Source: Kaufmann, D., A. Kraay and M. Mastruzzi 2006: Governance Matters V: Governance Indicators for 1996-2005

Democratic elections are one aspect of good governance

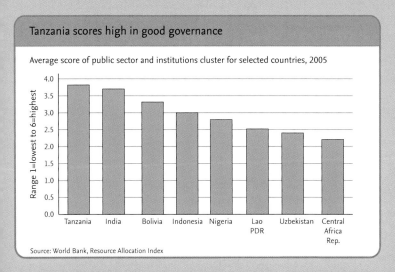

Tanzania scores high in good governance

Average score of public sector and institutions cluster for selected countries, 2005

Range 1=lowest to 6=highest

Countries: Tanzania, India, Bolivia, Indonesia, Nigeria, Lao PDR, Uzbekistan, Central Africa Rep.

Source: World Bank, Resource Allocation Index

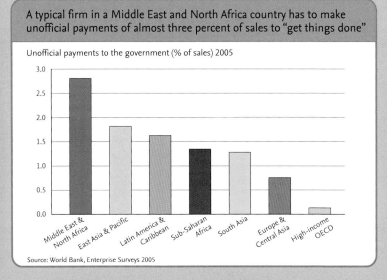

A typical firm in a Middle East and North Africa country has to make unofficial payments of almost three percent of sales to "get things done"

Unofficial payments to the government (% of sales) 2005

Regions: Middle East & North Africa, East Asia & Pacific, Latin America & Caribbean, Sub-Saharan Africa, South Asia, Europe & Central Asia, High-income OECD

Source: World Bank, Enterprise Surveys 2005

The World Bank's Country Policy and Institutional Assessment (CPIA) is an annual exercise by World Bank staff to measure the extent to which a country's policy and institutional framework supports sustainable growth and poverty reduction. Note that CPIA indicators examine policies and institutions, not development outcomes, which can depend on forces outside a country's control. There are 16 criteria grouped into four clusters; one of the clusters (shown in the chart on the left) is the public sector management and institutions cluster. This cluster includes five criteria: property rights and rule-based government, quality of budget and financial management, efficiency of revenue mobilization, quality of public administration, and transparency, accountability, and corruption in the public sector.

Parliament in session in South Africa

have to make unofficial payments to "get things done" with regard to customs, taxes, and licenses, and business managers have to spend too much time on red tape.

Measuring the quality of institutions and governance outcomes is difficult, and often subject to large margins of error. Data for one dimension of governance—control of corruption—are presented in the map. The data are an aggregate measure derived from several sources of informed views of individuals from both the private and public sector. The map represents data on control of corruption by quartiles, from the best performing (highest quartile) to the poorest performing (lowest quartile). Note that some developing countries have better scores on some governance measures than developed countries.

Controlling corruption

control of corruption from the Worldwide Governance
Indicators, percentile rank, 2005

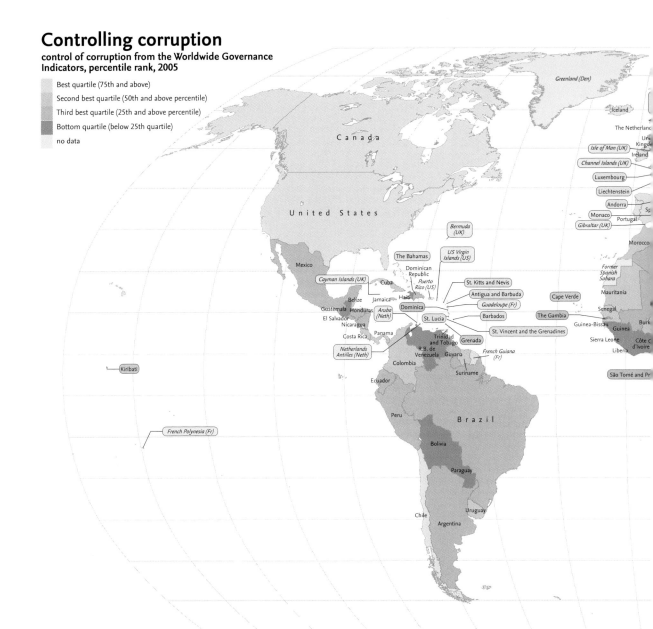

- Best quartile (75th and above)
- Second best quartile (50th and above percentile)
- Third best quartile (25th and above percentile)
- Bottom quartile (below 25th quartile)
- no data

People in many countries are fighting against corruption

Rank	Developing countries, population over 1 million	percentile rank, 2005
Control of corruption		
1	Chile	90
2	Botswana	82
3	Estonia	80
4	Bhutan	79
5	Uruguay	74
6	Oman	73
7	Hungary	70
8	South Africa	70
9	Slovak Republic	68
10	Czech Republic	68

Facts	Internet links	
Nine Sub-Saharan African countries rank in the second-best quartile in control of corruption.	► World Bank: Governance and Anti-Corruption	**www.govindicators.org**
Research shows that there is a relationship between lower levels of income and higher corruption, but some developing areas such as the Baltic states, Botswana, and Chile have reached high standards of governance without reaching the ranks of wealthy countries.	► World Bank: Enterprise Surveys	**www.enterprisesurveys.org**
	► World Bank: Doing Business	**www.doingbusiness.org**
Corruption is one of the most significant obstacles to doing business in many developing countries.	► UNDP: Democratic Governance	**www.undp.org/governance**
Countries that tackle corruption and improve rule of law can increase national incomes by as much as 4 times in the long term and child mortality can fall by as much as 75 percent.	► Transparency International	**www.transparency.org**

Economies have become increasingly dependent on each other for goods, services, labor, and capital. Advances in information and communications technology, expanding financial markets, and cheaper transportation systems have enabled easier movement of labor and capital between countries, accelerating global integration, but many barriers remain. The benefits from global integration need to be equitably shared among countries as well as within a country.

Traditional patterns of production and employment have given way to new modes of production and distribution processes spread over multiple locations. Developing countries are attracting foreign capital investment in manufacturing industries with higher returns. Skilled as well as unskilled labor is seeking employment in foreign countries in pursuit of higher wages. High-income economies are looking at the developing world to meet the increased demand for technology workers.

As the global economy becomes more integrated, the relative importance of trade has increased. Trade in goods was equal to 45 percent of global gross domestic product (GDP) in 2004, up from 32 percent in 1990.

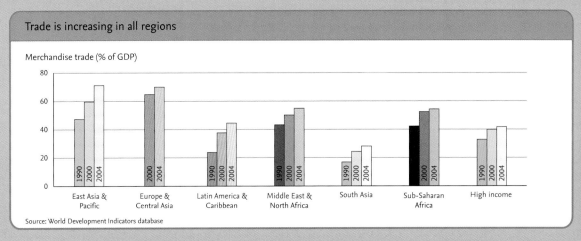

Trade is increasing in all regions

Merchandise trade (% of GDP)

Source: World Development Indicators database

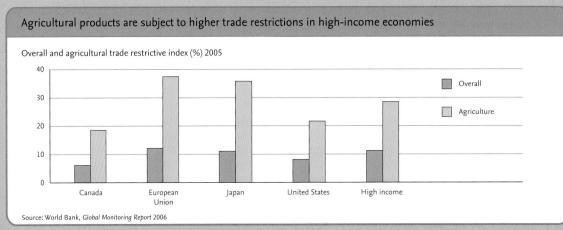

Agricultural products are subject to higher trade restrictions in high-income economies

Overall and agricultural trade restrictive index (%) 2005

Source: World Bank, *Global Monitoring Report 2006*

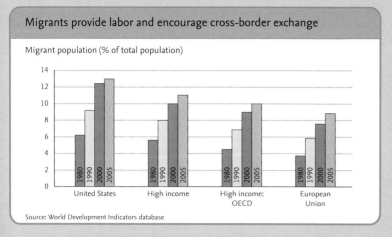

Migrants provide labor and encourage cross-border exchange

Migrant population (% of total population)

Source: World Development Indicators database

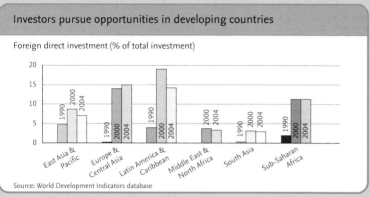

Investors pursue opportunities in developing countries

Foreign direct investment (% of total investment)

Source: World Development Indicators database

The export and import of goods continues to increase as the world becomes more integrated

Over the same period, trade in services increased from 8 percent to 11 percent of global GDP. But agricultural and industrial goods still dominate world trade, accounting for 80 percent of total trade (exports plus imports) in 2004.

While some developing countries, such as China and India, are making rapid progress as exporters of goods and services, the high-income economies still account for 72 percent of world merchandise exports, of which exports to the developing countries amounted to 16 percent in 2004. Between 1994 and 2004 merchandise exports of the high-income countries grew at 7.2 percent a year in nominal terms. Developing country exports grew at 11.5 percent a year during this period.

Reductions in tariff and non-tariff barriers have helped to spur trade, but many trade barriers remain. These barriers are costly to both consumers in developed countries and producers in developing countries. The poorest countries impose the most restrictions to protect their producers and raise revenues for their governments. But rich countries often impose their highest barriers on the exports of developing countries, especially agricultural products. Total agricultural support in OECD countries exceeded $385 billion in 2005, encouraging greater production in OECD countries and undercutting developing country producers.

Effective global integration includes the free flow of goods, services, investment, labor, and technology transfers, not just reduction of tariffs and import quotas. An open and equitable trading system enhances growth opportunities and encourages domestic and foreign investment. As countries have reduced restrictions on foreign investment, capital flows have increased, accounting for an increasing proportion of domestic investment.

Merchandise trade
exports and imports as a share of GDP, 2004

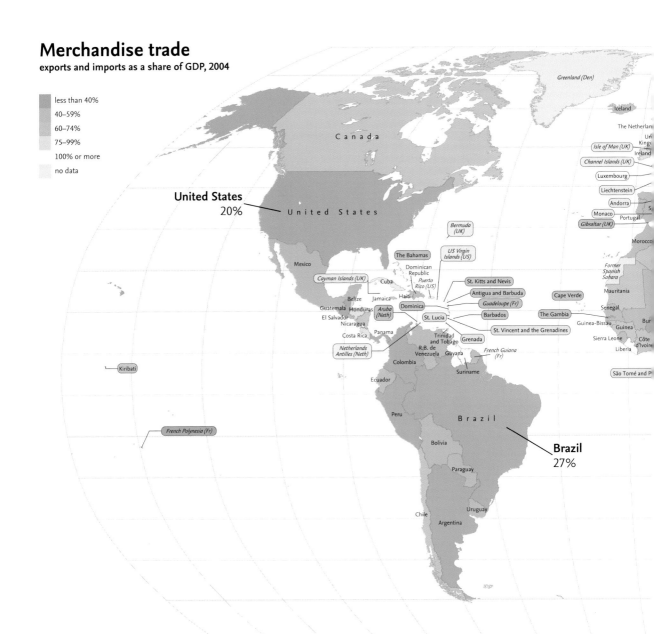

Legend:
- less than 40%
- 40–59%
- 60–74%
- 75–99%
- 100% or more
- no data

United States
20%

Brazil
27%

Singapore relies heavily on trade with the rest of the world	Merchandise trade

Merchandise trade

Rank	Developing countries	% of GDP 2004
1	Liberia	249
2	Malaysia	196
3	Equatorial Guinea	193
4	Guyana	162
5	Lesotho	156
6	Swaziland	153
7	Slovak Republic	139
8	Suriname	137
9	Belarus	131
10	Vietnam	129

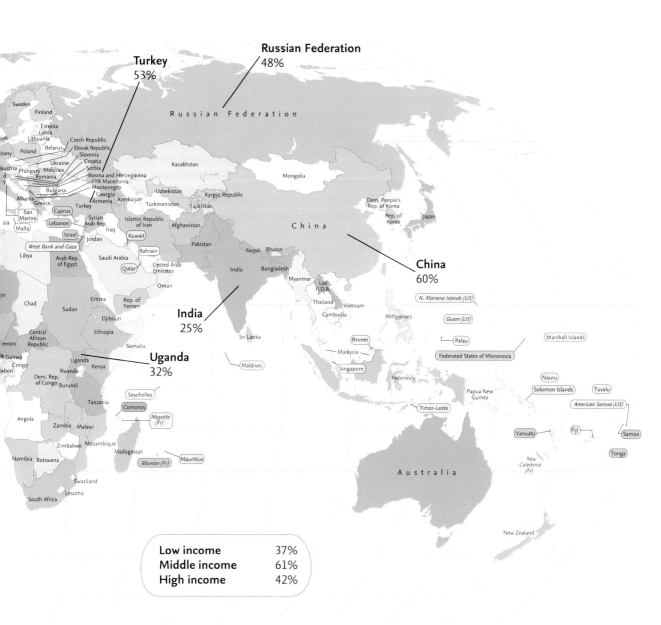

Low income	37%
Middle income	61%
High income	42%

Facts	Internet links	
Many small countries such as Singapore and Equatorial Guinea are highly dependent on trade. In 2004, Singapore's merchandise trade was more than 300 percent of its GDP.	▶ World Bank	**www.worldbank.org/trade**
The United States, with a merchandise trade to GDP ratio of only 20 percent, exports and imports more goods than any other country.	▶ Organisation for Economic Co-operation and Development	**www.oecd.org**
Cambodia increased its trade by more than 5 times in nominal terms between 1990 and 2004.	▶ International Monetary Fund	**www.imf.org**
38 countries had a lower ratio of trade to GDP in 2004 compared to 1990.	▶ World Trade Organization	**www.wto.org** (go to Resources, select Trade Statistics)
East Asia and Pacific region had the highest trade to GDP ratio, with 71 percent, whereas South Asia had the lowest, with 28 percent.	▶ United Nations Conference on Trade and Development	**www.unctad.org**

Trade in services

exports and imports of services as a share of GDP, 2004

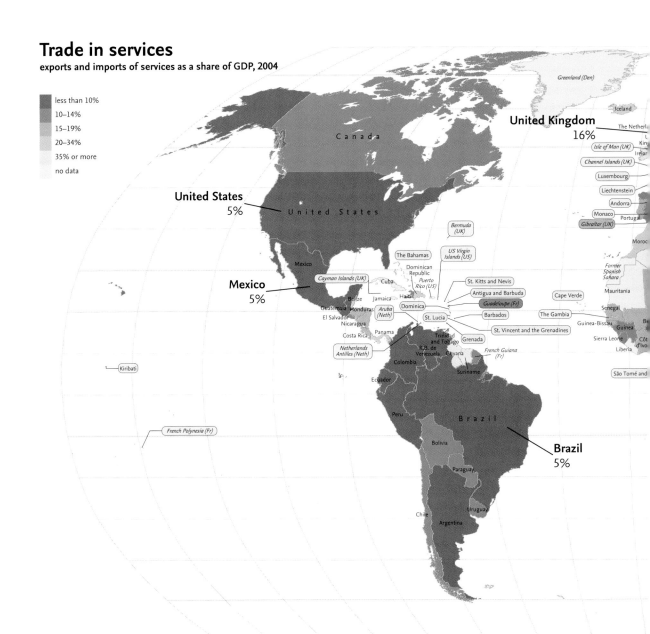

Legend:
- less than 10%
- 10–14%
- 15–19%
- 20–34%
- 35% or more
- no data

United Kingdom
16%

United States
5%

Mexico
5%

Brazil
5%

Map labels: Greenland (Den), Iceland, The Nether..., Isle of Man (UK), Ireland, Channel Islands (UK), Luxembourg, Liechtenstein, Andorra, Monaco, Portugal, Gibraltar (UK), Moroc..., Canada, United States, Bermuda (UK), US Virgin Islands (US), Former Spanish Sahara, Mauritania, The Bahamas, Dominican Republic, Puerto Rico (US), St. Kitts and Nevis, Cape Verde, Senegal, Cayman Islands (UK), Cuba, Haiti, Antigua and Barbuda, Guadeloupe (Fr), Mauritius, Mexico, Jamaica, Dominica, The Gambia, Belize, Aruba (Neth), St. Lucia, Barbados, Guinea-Bissau, Guinea, Guatemala, Honduras, St. Vincent and the Grenadines, El Salvador, Nicaragua, Trinidad and Tobago, Grenada, Sierra Leone, Côte d'Ivo..., Costa Rica, Panama, R.B. de Venezuela, Guyana, French Guiana (Fr), Liberia, Netherlands Antilles (Neth), Colombia, Suriname, São Tomé and..., Kiribati, Ecuador, Peru, Brazil, French Polynesia (Fr), Bolivia, Paraguay, Chile, Uruguay, Argentina

Trade in computer services is an increasingly important contribution to many countries' economies

Trade in services		
Rank	Developing countries	% of GD 2004
1	Maldives	83
2	Lebanon	82
3	Seychelles	76
4	Barbados	64
5	Vanuatu	56
6	Mongolia	52
7	Jamaica	45
8	Guyana	44
9	Mauritius	41
10	Swaziland	41

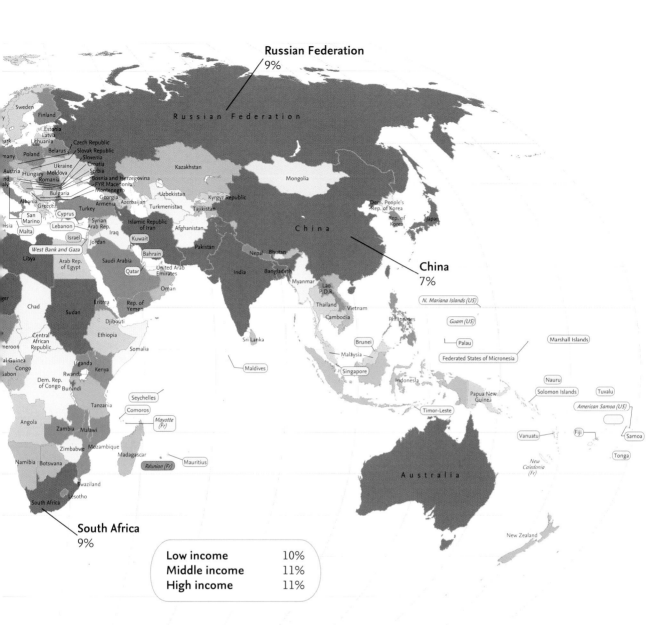

Russian Federation
9%

China
7%

South Africa
9%

Low income	10%
Middle income	11%
High income	11%

Facts	Internet links	
World exports of services grew from $815 million in 1990 to over $2 billion in 2004.	▶ World Bank	www.worldbank.org/trade
Developing countries increased their exports of services from $111 million in 1990 to $424 million in 2004.	▶ Organisation for Economic Co-operation and Development	www.oecd.org
Albania increased its trade in services by more than 20 times in nominal terms between 1990 and 2004.	▶ International Monetary Fund	www.imf.org
But 29 countries had a lower ratio of trade in services to GDP in 2004 compared to 1990.	▶ World Trade Organization	www.wto.org (go to Trade Topics, select Services Gateway)
Luxembourg had the highest ratio of trade in services to GDP (169 percent) in 2004.	▶ United Nations Conference on Trade and Development	www.unctad.org

Global integration has accelerated in recent years. More people are on the move. Countries are exchanging more goods and services. And international financial flows have grown. But even in an expanding world economy, many countries cannot finance their own development. Aid helps to fill the gap.

Nigeria is one of the many developing countries to benefit from debt relief

Development is a partnership between developing and donor countries. Donor countries help recipient countries build capacity to foster change. And recipient countries invest in their people and create an environment that sustains growth.

Countries that have difficulty tapping financial markets must rely largely on aid flows from wealthier countries to fund development programs. In 2005 developing countries received official development assistance (ODA) and official aid totaling approximately $106.5 billion, up from $79.6 billion in 2004 and $53.7 billion in 2000. Debt relief to Afghanistan, Iraq, and Nigeria and tsunami relief to countries in East Asia and

Pacific accounted for a large part of the increases in 2004 and 2005.

Who were the largest donors? According to the Organisation for Economic Co-operation and Development's (OECD) Development Assistance Committee (DAC), in 2005, the top ten donors contributed 86 percent of total ODA from DAC members. The top four – the United States, Japan, the United Kingdom, and France – contributed more than half.

If measured as a share of donors' gross national income (GNI), aid declined sharply in the 1990s but started growing again after

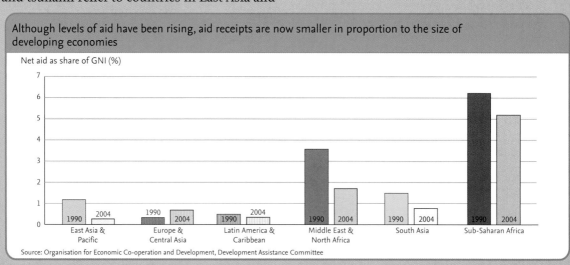

Although levels of aid have been rising, aid receipts are now smaller in proportion to the size of developing economies

Net aid as share of GNI (%)

East Asia & Pacific | Europe & Central Asia | Latin America & Caribbean | Middle East & North Africa | South Asia | Sub-Saharan Africa
(bars shown for 1990 and 2004)

Source: Organisation for Economic Co-operation and Development, Development Assistance Committee

Aid commitments after the G-8 meeting at Gleneagles, Scotland						
	2004		**2010 projection**			
	Net ODA ($millions)	ODA/GNI (%)	Net ODA ($millions)	ODA/GNI (%)	Real change in ODA compared with 2004 Amount ($millions)	(%)
Denmark	2,037	0.85	2,185	0.80	148	7
France	8,473	0.41	14,110	0.61	5,638	67
Germany	7,534	0.28	15,509	0.51	7,975	106
Italy	2,462	0.15	9,262	0.51	6,801	276
Luxembourg	236	0.83	328	1.00	93	39
Netherlands	4,204	0.73	5,070	0.80	867	21
Spain	2,437	0.24	6,925	0.59	4,488	184
Sweden	2,722	0.78	4,025	1.00	1,303	48
United Kingdom	7,883	0.36	14,600	0.59	6,717	85
Other EU members[a]	4,899	0.36	9,206	0.60	4,306	88
EU members, total	**42,886**	**0.35**	**81,221**	**0.59**	**38,335**	**89**
Canada	2,599	0.27	3,648	0.33	1,049	40
Japan	8,906	0.19	11,906	0.22	3,000	34
Norway	2,199	0.87	2,876	1.00	677	31
United States	19,705	0.17	24,000	0.18	4,295	22
Other DAC members[b]	3,218	0.30	4,477	0.37	1,260	39
DAC members, total	**79,512**	**0.26**	**128,128**	**0.36**	**48,616**	**61**

a. Austria, Belgium, Finland, Greece, Ireland and Portugal b. Australia, New Zealand, and Switzerland
Source: OECD Journal on Development 2006

2000. Only five donor countries have fulfilled the UN official development assistance target of 0.7 percent of GNI: Denmark, Luxembourg, the Netherlands, Norway, and Sweden. As donor countries follow through on their promises at the United Nations International Conference on Financing for Development, in Monterrey, Mexico, in 2002 and at the more recent Group of Eight (G-8) summit at Gleneagles, Scotland, aid has hit a record high. But a large part of this came as debt relief, not new aid flows.

A substantial increase in aid flows—together with private capital flows—will be required to help developing countries achieve the Millennium Development Goals. This is especially true for the countries of Sub-Saharan Africa, where aid is the largest source of external finance. Aid received by Sub-Saharan African countries declined during the 1990s from more than 6 percent of gross domestic product (GDP) to 4 percent, but it has since increased to 5 percent.

Official development assistance (ODA) is on the rise

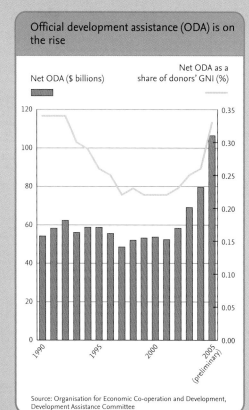

Net ODA ($ billions)

Net ODA as a share of donors' GNI (%)

Source: Organisation for Economic Co-operation and Development, Development Assistance Committee

Who were the largest donors in 2005?

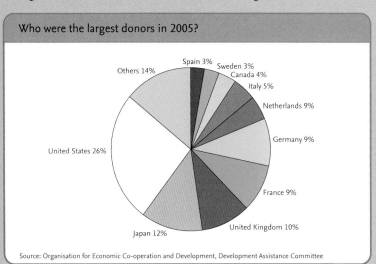

Others 14%
Spain 3%
Sweden 3%
Canada 4%
Italy 5%
Netherlands 9%
Germany 9%
France 9%
United Kingdom 10%
Japan 12%
United States 26%

Source: Organisation for Economic Co-operation and Development, Development Assistance Committee

Different sources of finance for developing countries

Selected net flows, 2004 ($ billions)

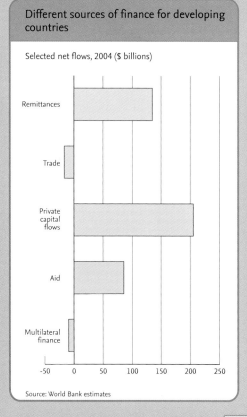

Remittances
Trade
Private capital flows
Aid
Multilateral finance

Source: World Bank estimates

Aid

aid per capita, 2004

received	donated
$75 or more	$200 or more
$30–75	$100–200
$15–29	$50–99
less than $15	Less than $50
net repayer	
no data	

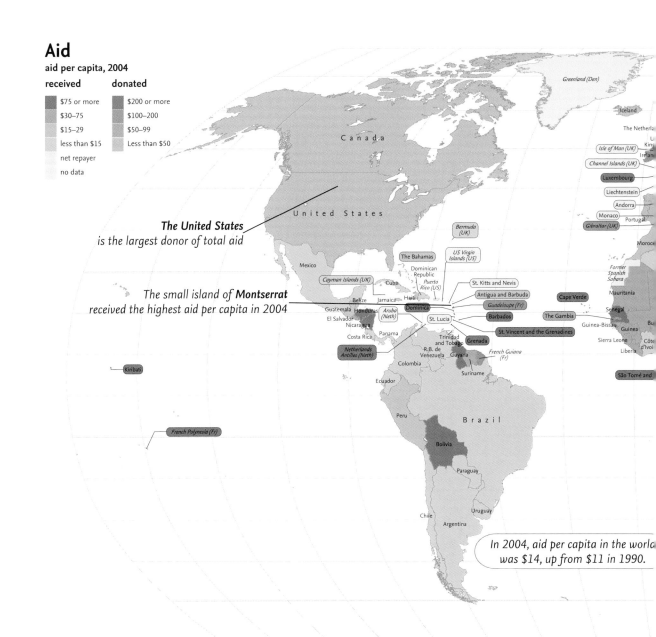

The United States *is the largest donor of total aid*

*The small island of **Montserrat** received the highest aid per capita in 2004*

In 2004, aid per capita in the world was $14, up from $11 in 1990.

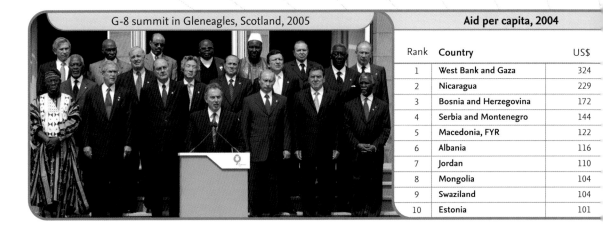

G-8 summit in Gleneagles, Scotland, 2005

Aid per capita, 2004

Rank	Country	US$
1	West Bank and Gaza	324
2	Nicaragua	229
3	Bosnia and Herzegovina	172
4	Serbia and Montenegro	144
5	Macedonia, FYR	122
6	Albania	116
7	Jordan	110
8	Mongolia	104
9	Swaziland	104
10	Estonia	101

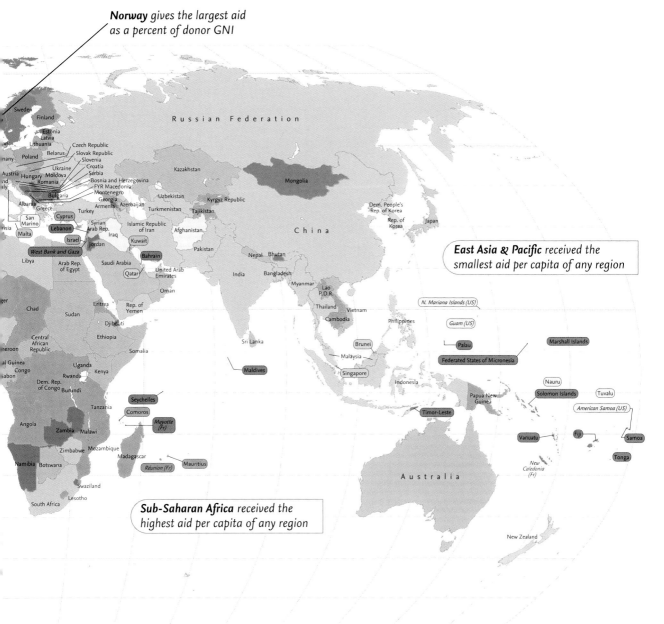

Norway gives the largest aid as a percent of donor GNI

East Asia & Pacific received the smallest aid per capita of any region

Sub-Saharan Africa received the highest aid per capita of any region

Facts	Internet links	
Official development assistance to developing countries from member countries of the OECD's Development Assistance Committee rose to $106.5 billion in 2005 — a record high.	▶ Organisation for Economic Co-operation and Development	www.oecd.org
Official development assistance represents 0.33 percent of the Development Assistance Committee members' combined gross national income in 2005, up from 0.26 percent in 2004.	▶ World Bank	www.worldbank.org
In 1950–1955, net aid was $1.95 billion.	▶ International Monetary Fund	www.imf.org
Since 1990, aid per capita increased by $17 in Europe & Central Asia (from $8 to $25). Aid to the Middle East and North Africa fell by $11 during the same period, from $46 to $35.	▶ The European Commission	ec.europa.eu/europeaid

Many countries borrow from abroad to finance development, but when debt exceeds the capacity of a country to service it, the debt burden becomes unsustainable and hinders development. Making debt manageable for poor countries is central to their efforts to achieve the Millennium Development Goals.

Debt owed by developing countries to foreign creditors emerged as a major issue in the late 1970s. The size of the debt and their ability to repay it was a problem for some Latin American countries in the 1980s and, in the 1990s, for many countries in Africa, East Asia, Latin America and Russia.

In 2004 the external debt of the developing countries amounted to 2.8 trillion dollars with the top 10 countries accounting for 57 percent of the debt. It has been increasing in most of the regions with the exception of the Middle East and North Africa, where debt declined slightly, and Sub-Saharan Africa, where it has remained at the 1995 level. Total debt service paid by developing countries was $450 billion in 2004. However, their debt burden measured by the ratio of debt service to exports, fell from a high 27 percent in 1999 to 14 percent in 2004. The ratio of total external debt to gross domestic product (GDP) declined from nearly 43 percent to 33 percent during this period.

The debt crisis of the 1980s and 1990s was the result of excessive borrowing with overly optimistic expectations. But cyclical

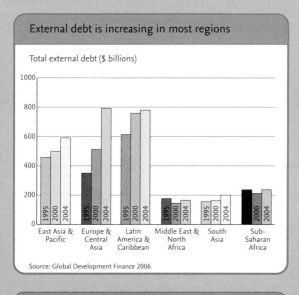

External debt is increasing in most regions

Total external debt ($ billions)

Source: Global Development Finance 2006

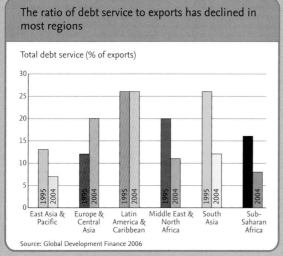

The ratio of debt service to exports has declined in most regions

Total debt service (% of exports)

Source: Global Development Finance 2006

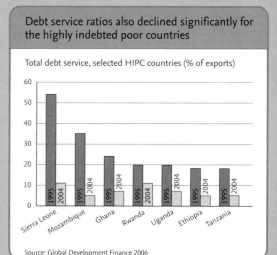

Debt service ratios also declined significantly for the highly indebted poor countries

Total debt service, selected HIPC countries (% of exports)

Source: Global Development Finance 2006

Mozambique, one of the Heavily Indebted Poor Countries, also qualifies for further debt stock cancellation

global recessions, declining agricultural commodity prices, bad governance and economic mismanagement, and internal and external conflicts left many poor countries unable to service their external debt. Some countries continued to borrow to meet their outstanding obligations, which only added to their burden in the absence of sustained output and export growth. Traditional debt relief, based on rescheduling and restructuring of payments, was insufficient to meet the needs of the poorest countries.

Special programs to address the problems of the poor countries with predominantly official creditors were started. In 1996 the World Bank and the International Monetary Fund (IMF) launched the Heavily Indebted Poor Countries (HIPC) initiative to provide relief to a group of mostly African countries with recurring debt repayment problems. The initiative aims to provide permanent relief from unsustainable debt by redirecting the resources going towards debt service to social expenditures aimed at poverty reduction. The HIPC initiative will provide a nominal debt service relief of over $61 billion for 29 countries.

Further, the International Development Association (IDA), the IMF, and African Development Fund have committed to cancel an additional debt stock of $49 billion for all HIPC countries under the new Multilateral Debt Relief Initiative (MDRI). The IDA and IMF have cancelled $27 billion and $3 billion debt stock respectively for 19 countries which have made progress in their economic and social reforms as agreed to with the World Bank and IMF under the HIPC initiative as of July 1, 2006.

Internal conflict can add to a country's debt obligation

External debt

debt service as share of exports, 2004

- 20% or more
- 15–19%
- 10–14%
- 5–9%
- less than 5%
- no data

Mexico
23%

Brazil
47%

Argentina
28%

Turkey is one of the top ten debtor countries

Top ten debtors in 2004

Rank	Country	Total external debt ($ billion)
1	China	249
2	Brazil	222
3	Russian Federation	197
4	Argentina	169
5	Turkey	162
6	Indonesia	141
7	Mexico	139
8	India	123
9	Poland	99
10	Hungary	63

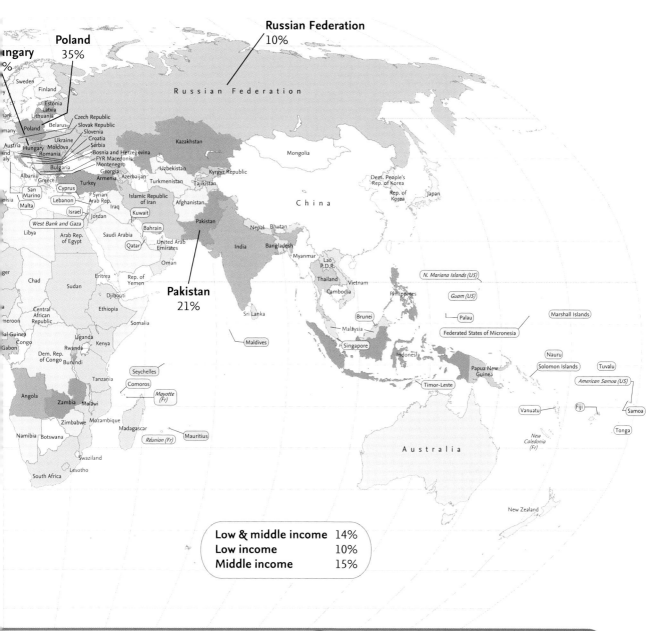

Hungary
%

Poland
35%

Russian Federation
10%

Russian Federation

Pakistan
21%

Low & middle income	14%
Low income	10%
Middle income	15%

Facts	Internet links	
For the 26 Heavily Indebted Poor Countries (HIPC) the ratio of debt service to exports fell from 15.1 percent in 1999 to 6.5 percent in 2005.	▶ Bank for International Settlements	**www.bis.org**
The gains are expected to continue through 2008. It is projected that HIPC debt service ratios will fall to 3.2 percent by 2008.	▶ World Bank	**www.worldbank.org/debt**
As a percentage of government revenue, debt service fell from 21.8 percent to 11.7 percent for HIPC, between 1999 and 2005.	▶ Organisation for Economic Co-operation and Development	**www.oecd.org**
The HIPC initiative has contributed to an increase in poverty-reducing expenditures in the HIPC which rose from 41.6 percent to 49.9 percent of government revenue between 1999 and 2005.	▶ International Monetary Fund	**www.imf.org**
The cost of the HIPC initiative for creditors in net present value terms is estimated to be $41.3 billion at the end of 2005.	▶ Joint External Debt Hub	**www.jedh.org**

Cities can be tremendously efficient. It is easier to provide water and sanitation services to people living closer together in urban settings than in dispersed rural communities. Access to health, education, and other social and cultural services is also much more readily available. However, as cities grow, the cost of meeting basic needs increases, as does the demand on the environment and natural resources.

Cities, now home to almost half the world's people, are growing rapidly in size and number, especially in developing countries. People flock to cities for work, access to public services, and a higher standard of living. In 2004 there were 20 megacities with populations of more than 10 million. Among developing countries, urbanization has gone farthest in Latin America, where 77 percent of the people live in urban areas. South Asia remains rural by comparison, with only 28 percent of its people in urban areas. (Definitions of urban areas vary by country and may not be fully comparable.) By 2030, 60 percent of the world's people will live in urban areas, in some countries ballooning beyond the capacity of the environment to support them adequately. The resulting

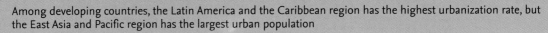

Among developing countries, the Latin America and the Caribbean region has the highest urbanization rate, but the East Asia and Pacific region has the largest urban population

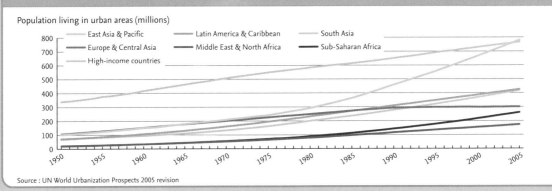

Population living in urban areas (millions)

Legend: East Asia & Pacific — Latin America & Caribbean — South Asia — Europe & Central Asia — Middle East & North Africa — Sub-Saharan Africa — High-income countries

Source : UN World Urbanization Prospects 2005 revision

High concentrations of airborne particulate matter (PM10) are often found in urban areas

Countries with the lowest level of PM10 concentrations in 2002	Urban-population weighted PM10 (microgram per cubic meter)	Countries with the highest level of PM10 concentrations in 2002	Urban-population weighted PM10 (microgram per cubic meter)
Belarus	9	Sudan	219
Papua New Guinea	11	Iraq	167
R.B. de Venezuela	12	Pakistan	165
Gabon	13	Bangladesh	157
Sweden	14	Uruguay	154
France	15	The Gambia	138

Source: World Bank estimates based on the study *Ambient Particulate Matter Concentrations in Residential and Pollution Hotspot Areas of World Cities: New Estimates Based on the Global Model of Ambient Particulates* (GMAPS), 2006

In slum areas lack of hygiene and sanitation ensures that water-borne diseases are rife

environmental consequences are poor living conditions, especially with the growth of slums, destruction of habitat, and water and air pollution.

Urbanization and the environment

Urbanization by itself is not an environmental issue, but urban environmental problems are a result of urban life. The cost of urbanization to human health comes from a variety of sources. Diarrheal diseases from inadequate sanitation account for an estimated 4 percent of the global burden of disease. The proximity to industrial works and roadways and the use of inefficient and polluting sources of energy can result in exposure to high levels of soot and small particles (PM10—fine, suspended particulates less than 10 microns in diameter) and contribute to respiratory diseases, lung cancer, and heart disease.

Air and water pollution in many of the world's major cities cause moderate to severe sickness and death, and cost billions of dollars in lost productivity and damages. Although all the world's megacities share these problems, water pollution tends to be most serious in south, southeast, and central Asia, and air pollution has the biggest impact in China, Latin America, and eastern Europe. Not only are the human and financial costs of pollution large, they tend to fall disproportionately on poor people, so addressing pollution is justified on equity grounds as well as on economic and environmental grounds.

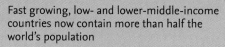
Fast growing, low- and lower-middle-income countries now contain more than half the world's population

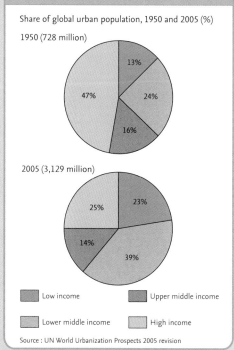
Share of global urban population, 1950 and 2005 (%)

1950 (728 million)

2005 (3,129 million)

Low income   Upper middle income
Lower middle income   High income

Source : UN World Urbanization Prospects 2005 revision

Particulate matter concentration levels of low- and lower-middle-income countries are significantly higher than those of the high-income countries

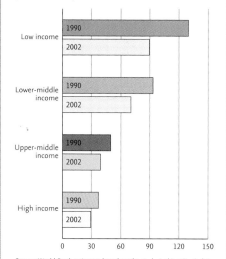
Particulate matter concentration, 1990 and 2002 (Urban-population weighted PM10 micrograms per cubic meter)

Source: World Bank estimates based on the study Ambient Particulate Matter Concentrations in Residential and Pollution Hotspot Areas of World Cities: New Estimates Based on the Global Model of Ambient Particulates (GMAPS), 2006

Urbanization

urban population as share of total population, 2005

- less than 35%
- 35–49%
- 50–64%
- 65–79%
- 80% or more
- no data

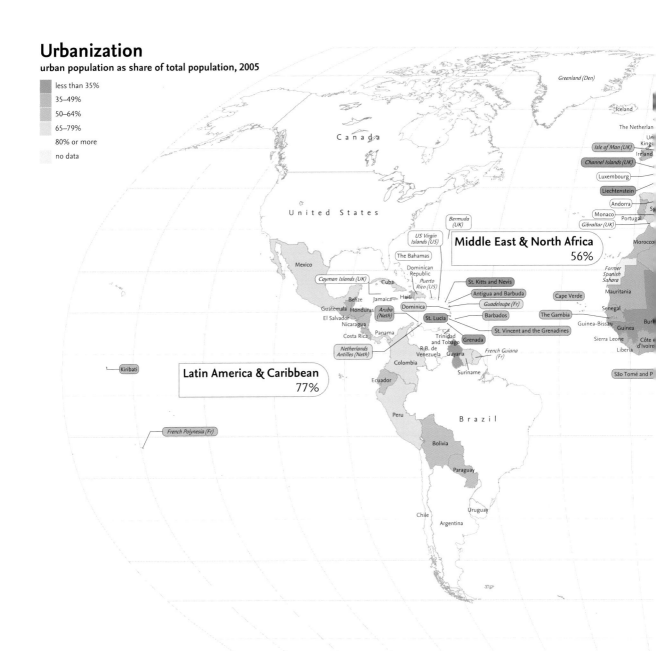

Middle East & North Africa
56%

Latin America & Caribbean
77%

Greenland (Den)

Iceland

The Netherlan

Un
Kingo

Isle of Man (UK)

Ireland

Channel Islands (UK)

Luxembourg

Liechtenstein

Andorra

Monaco

Portugal

Gibraltar (UK)

Canada

United States

Bermuda
(UK)

US Virgin
Islands (US)

The Bahamas

Dominican
Republic

Mexico

Cayman Islands (UK)

Cuba

Puerto
Rico (US)

Belize

Jamaica

Haiti

Guatemala

Honduras

Aruba
(Neth)

Dominica

El Salvador

Nicaragua

Costa Rica

Panama

Netherlands
Antilles (Neth)

St. Kitts and Nevis

Antigua and Barbuda

Guadeloupe (Fr)

St. Lucia

Barbados

St. Vincent and the Grenadines

Trinidad
and Tobago

Grenada

R.B. de
Venezuela

Colombia

Guyana

French Guiana
(Fr)

Suriname

Ecuador

Peru

Brazil

Bolivia

Paraguay

Chile

Uruguay

Argentina

Kiribati

French Polynesia (Fr)

Morocco

Former
Spanish
Sahara

Mauritania

Cape Verde

Senegal

The Gambia

Guinea-Bissau

Guinea

Sierra Leone

Côte
d'Ivoire

Liberia

São Tomé and P

Bur

Mumbai, India, is one of the fastest growing cities
in the developing world

10 least urbanized countries

Rank	Country	Urbanization of total popul
1	Burundi	10.0
2	Bhutan	11.1
3	Trinidad and Tobago	12.2
4	Uganda	12.6
5	Papua New Guinea	13.4
6	Liechtenstein	14.6
7	Sri Lanka	15.1
8	Nepal	15.8
9	Ethiopia	16.0
10	Niger	16.8

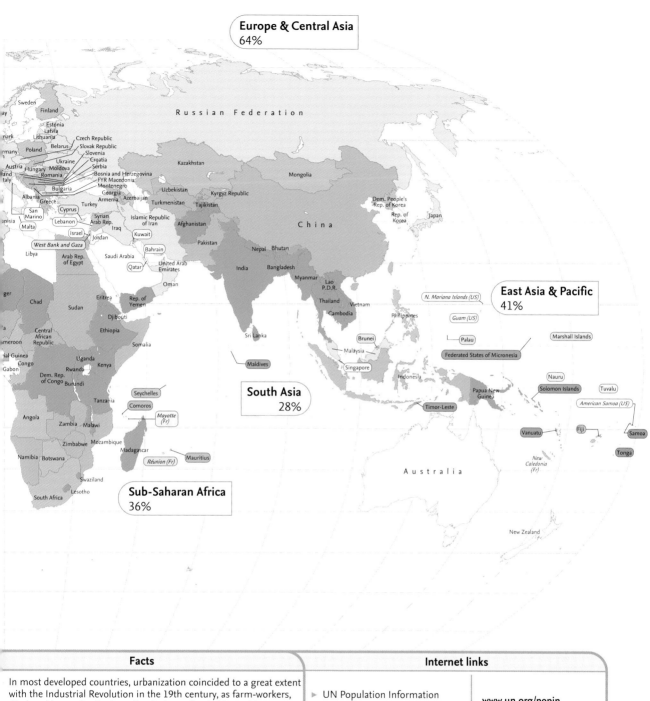

Europe & Central Asia
64%

Russian Federation

Sweden
Finland
Estonia
Latvia
Lithuania
Czech Republic
Poland
Belarus
Slovak Republic
Slovenia
Croatia
Ukraine
Hungary Moldova
Serbia
Bosnia and Herzegovina
FYR Macedonia
Montenegro
Bulgaria
Georgia
Albania
Armenia Azerbaijan
Greece
Turkey
Cyprus
Syrian
Arab Rep.
Lebanon
Israel
Jordan
West Bank and Gaza
Libya
Arab Rep.
of Egypt
Saudi Arabia
Qatar
United Arab
Emirates
Oman

Kazakhstan
Mongolia
Uzbekistan
Kyrgyz Republic
Turkmenistan
Tajikistan
Islamic Republic
of Iran
Afghanistan
Iraq
Kuwait
Bahrain
Pakistan
Nepal Bhutan
India
Bangladesh
Myanmar

Dem. People's
Rep. of Korea
Rep. of
Korea
Japan

C h i n a

Niger
Chad
Central
African
Republic
Cameroon
Eritrea
Sudan
Djibouti
Ethiopia
Somalia
Rep. of
Yemen
Sri Lanka

Lao
P.D.R.
Thailand
Vietnam
Cambodia
Philippines

East Asia & Pacific
41%

N. Mariana Islands (US)
Guam (US)
Palau
Marshall Islands
Federated States of Micronesia

Brunei
Malaysia
Singapore
Indonesia

Maldives

South Asia
28%

Eq. Guinea
Congo
Gabon
Dem. Rep.
of Congo
Uganda
Rwanda
Burundi
Kenya
Tanzania
Seychelles
Comoros
Mayotte
(Fr)

Nauru
Solomon Islands
Tuvalu
American Samoa (US)

Papua New
Guinea
Timor-Leste

Angola
Zambia Malawi
Zimbabwe Mozambique
Namibia Botswana
Madagascar
Réunion (Fr)
Mauritius
Swaziland
South Africa Lesotho

Vanuatu
Fiji
Samoa
Tonga

A u s t r a l i a

New
Caledonia
(Fr)

Sub-Saharan Africa
36%

New Zealand

Facts	Internet links	
In most developed countries, urbanization coincided to a great extent with the Industrial Revolution in the 19th century, as farm-workers, displaced by mechanization of agriculture, flooded into cities.	► UN Population Information Network	www.un.org/popin
In 2001, 924 million people were living in slums worldwide; at present growth rates of urbanization, about 2 billion people will be living in slums in 2030.	► Population Reference Bureau	www.prb.org
In Latin America, the share of urban population is as high as in high-income Europe.		
The world's urban population is expected to rise to 5 billion by 2030.	► World Bank–Urban development	www.worldbank.org/urban

Particulate matter

urban-population weighted PM10,
micrograms per cubic meter, 2002

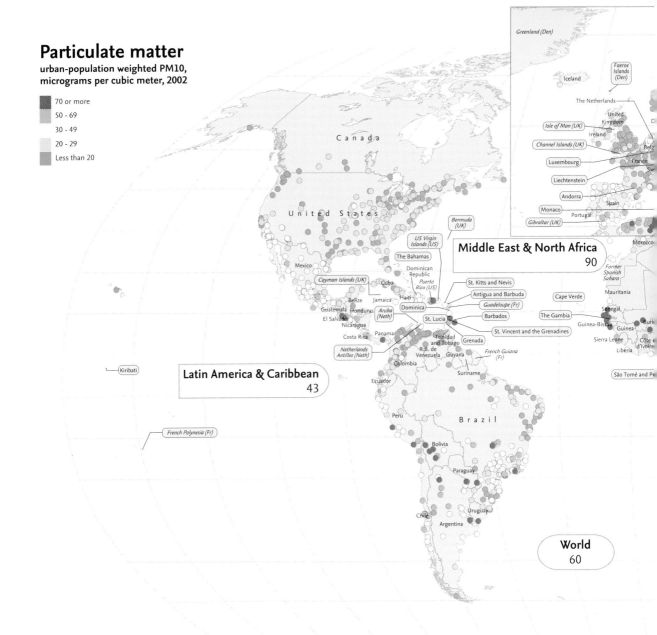

- 70 or more
- 50 - 69
- 30 - 49
- 20 - 29
- Less than 20

Middle East & North Africa
90

Latin America & Caribbean
43

World
60

Traffic is a major contributor to urban air pollution

Cities with the highest level of particulate ma

Rank	City, Country	Particulate ma micrograms p cubic meter
1	Nyala, Sudan	318
2=	Omdurman, Sudan	255
2=	Kano, Nigeria	255
4	Khartoum, Sudan	238
5=	Maroua, Cameroon	232
5=	Medani, Sudan	232
7	Garoua, Cameroon	228
8	Kassala, Sudan	227
9=	El Obeid, Sudan	224
9=	Kaduna, Nigeria	224

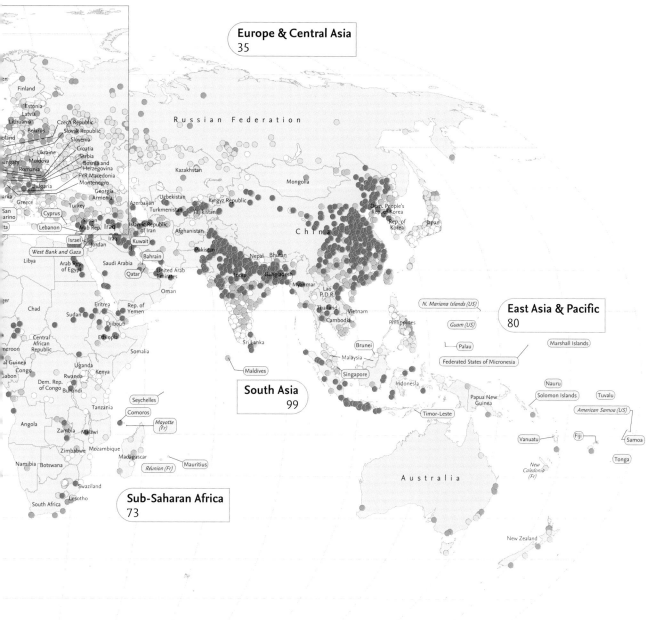

Europe & Central Asia
35

East Asia & Pacific
80

South Asia
99

Sub-Saharan Africa
73

Facts	Internet links	
The world's urban-population weighted particulate matter concentrations (PM10) are estimated at 60 micrograms per cubic meter in 2002.	▶ World Bank – Environment	econ.worldbank.org/ environment
Particulate matter concentration has decreased globally and in all the regions and income groups between 1990 and 2002.		
Nine out of ten countries with the highest levels of PM10 concentrations are among the lower-income economies.	▶ World Bank	www.worldbank.org (search for PM10)
Particulate matter concentration levels in low-income countries were three times those of the high income countries in 2002.	▶ U.S. Environmental Protection Agency	www.epa.gov/oar/aqtrnd97/ brochure/pm10.html
The ten cities with the lowest level of particulate matter are located in Venezuela and Belarus.		

Over the past 25 years agricultural output has grown more rapidly than population, diminishing concerns of a global food shortage. But malnutrition and food shortages take a pervasive toll in developing countries, especially in Sub-Saharan Africa. Meeting the growing demand for food and improving the quality of life of those who depend on land for their subsistence requires increasing the productivity of farmers and their land.

By 2050 there will be 9 billion people living on earth, almost 3 billion more than today. Most will live in cities, but all will depend upon rural areas to feed them. Although the amount of arable land per capita has declined in most developing countries, yields have increased. In the past 25 years, the food supply has expanded faster than population, and there is every reason to think that it will continue to do so. But in Sub-Saharan Africa, with some of the highest rates of undernourishment, food production has barely kept pace with population increase. Intensified cultivation through the use of fertilizers, pesticides, irrigation, and new plant varieties, can make limited land more productive but may also worsen environmental degradation, while expansion into new lands destroys natural habitats and decreases biological diversity. The effects of climate change represent a further challenge to efforts to raise the productivity of plants and animals.

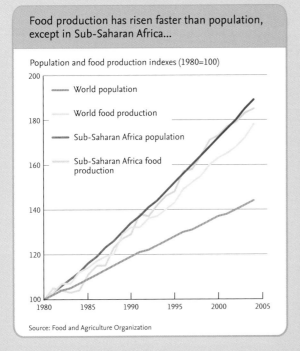

Food production has risen faster than population, except in Sub-Saharan Africa...

Population and food production indexes (1980=100)

- World population
- World food production
- Sub-Saharan Africa population
- Sub-Saharan Africa food production

Source: Food and Agriculture Organization

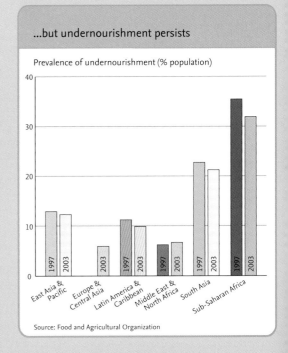

...but undernourishment persists

Prevalence of undernourishment (% population)

East Asia & Pacific · Europe & Central Asia · Latin America & Caribbean · Middle East & North Africa · South Asia · Sub-Saharan Africa

Source: Food and Agricultural Organization

Overgrazing is one of many causes of land degradation

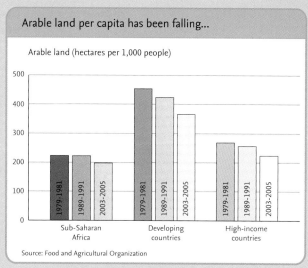

Arable land per capita has been falling...

Arable land (hectares per 1,000 people)

Sub-Saharan Africa · Developing countries · High-income countries

1979-1981 · 1989-1991 · 2003-2005

Source: Food and Agricultural Organization

Many poor farmers subsist on fragile lands, poorly suited to intensive farming. They lack access to fertilizers, farm equipment, irrigation systems, high yielding plant varieties, and markets for their produce. Overgrazing, deforestation, improper crop rotation, and poor soil and water management contribute to land degradation. The degradation of land reduces its productivity, encouraging growing populations to move on to new and poorer land, converting forests and fragile, semi-arid areas into low-productivity cultivated areas.

In 2002, almost 1.4 billion people were living on fragile lands, more than three-quarters of them in Asia and Africa, where yields are low, the risks of crop failure are high, and a large portion of the population is undernourished. Many, especially in Africa, are vulnerable to climate variability and associated floods and droughts that are likely to become more pronounced as a result of climate change, leading to local famines and increased levels of malnutrition. Sustainable production methods, based on environmentally sound practices, along with the development of more efficient markets for farm inputs and outputs and off-farm activities, are the key to improving rural livelihoods and expanding the global food supply.

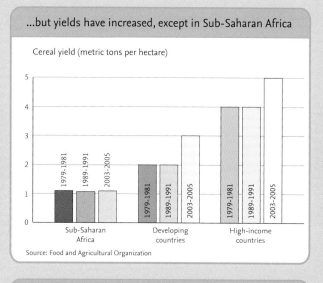

...but yields have increased, except in Sub-Saharan Africa

Cereal yield (metric tons per hectare)

Sub-Saharan Africa · Developing countries · High-income countries

1979-1981 · 1989-1991 · 2003-2005

Source: Food and Agricultural Organization

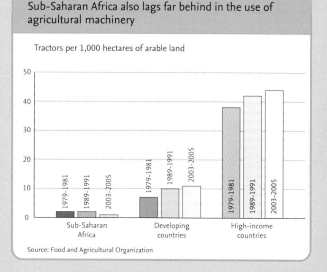

Sub-Saharan Africa also lags far behind in the use of agricultural machinery

Tractors per 1,000 hectares of arable land

Sub-Saharan Africa · Developing countries · High-income countries

1979-1981 · 1989-1991 · 2003-2005

Source: Food and Agricultural Organization

Arable land

hectares per capita, 2001-2003

less than 0.10
0.10-0.19
0.20-0.29
0.30-0.49
0.50 or more
no data

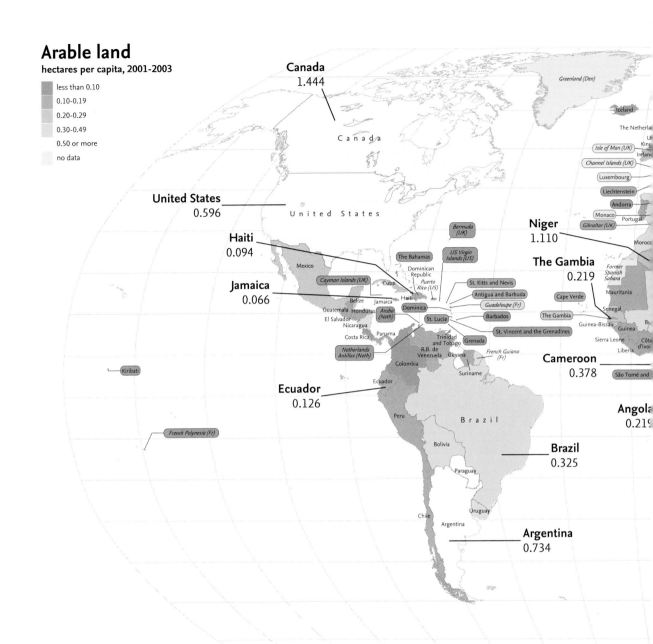

Canada
1.444

Greenland (Den)

Iceland

The Netherla

Isle of Man (UK)

Channel Islands (UK)

Luxembourg

Liechtenstein

Andorra

Monaco Portugal

Gibraltar (UK)

United States
0.596

United States

Niger
1.110

Morocc

Haiti
0.094

Bermuda (UK)

The Bahamas

US Virgin Islands (US)

Mexico

Dominican Republic

Puerto Rico (US)

Cuba

Haiti

The Gambia
0.219

Former Spanish Sahara

Mauritania

Senegal

Jamaica
0.066

Cayman Islands (UK)

Belize

Jamaica

St. Kitts and Nevis

Antigua and Barbuda

Guadeloupe (Fr)

Dominica

Cape Verde

The Gambia

Guinea-Bissau

Guinea

Guatemala Honduras *Aruba (Neth)*

El Salvador

Nicaragua

St. Lucia

Barbados

Sierra Leone

Côte d'Ivoi

Costa Rica Panama

Netherlands Antilles (Neth)

Colombia

Trinidad and Tobago

R.B. de Venezuela

Grenada

St. Vincent and the Grenadines

Guyana

French Guiana (Fr)

Liberia

Cameroon
0.378

São Tomé and

Kiribati

Ecuador
0.126

Ecuador

Suriname

Peru

B r a z i l

Angola
0.219

French Polynesia (Fr)

Bolivia

Brazil
0.325

Paraguay

Chile

Uruguay

Argentina

Argentina
0.734

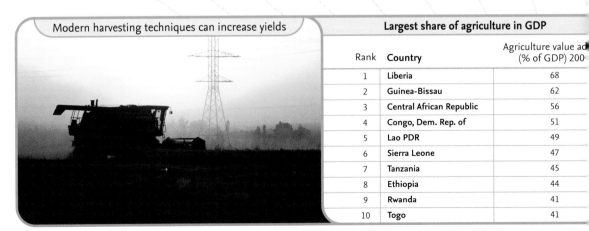

Modern harvesting techniques can increase yields

Largest share of agriculture in GDP

Rank	Country	Agriculture value ad (% of GDP) 200
1	Liberia	68
2	Guinea-Bissau	62
3	Central African Republic	56
4	Congo, Dem. Rep. of	51
5	Lao PDR	49
6	Sierra Leone	47
7	Tanzania	45
8	Ethiopia	44
9	Rwanda	41
10	Togo	41

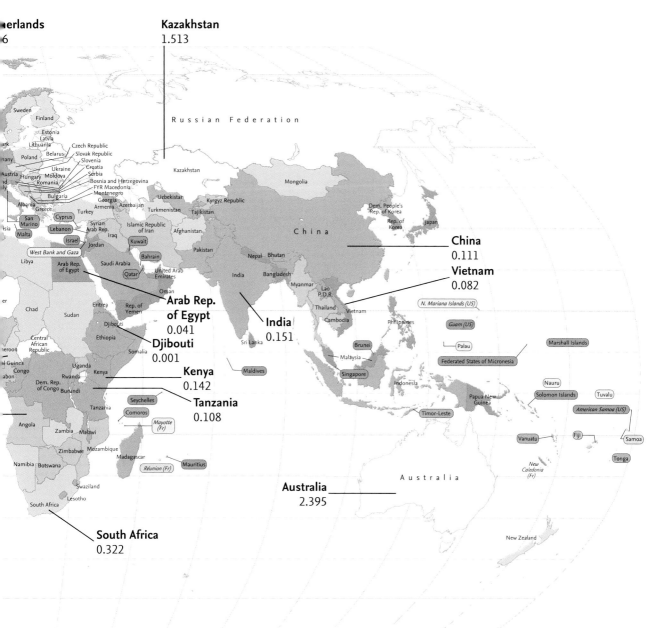

Facts	Internet links	
Arable land areas of the world comprise approximately 11 percent of the total land area.	▶ Food and Agriculture Organization	**www.fao.org/default.aspx**
Europe and Central Asia, with 0.57 hectares per person, has the highest arable land available per capita.		
Over the past two decades arable land per capita has declined by 19 percent in low income countries.	▶ International Food Policy Research Institute	**www.ifpri.org**
During the past 30 years, Africa has experienced at least one major drought each decade.		
The world's total arable land area is 1.4 billion hectares.	▶ Consultative Group on International Agricultural Research	**www.cgiar.org**
Fertilizer use per hectare is highest in East Asia and Pacific and lowest (by a factor of 17) in Sub-Saharan Africa.		

Undernourishment

prevalence of undernourishment,
share of population, average, 2001-2003

- 30% or more
- 20-29%
- 10-19%
- 5-9%
- less than 5%
- no data

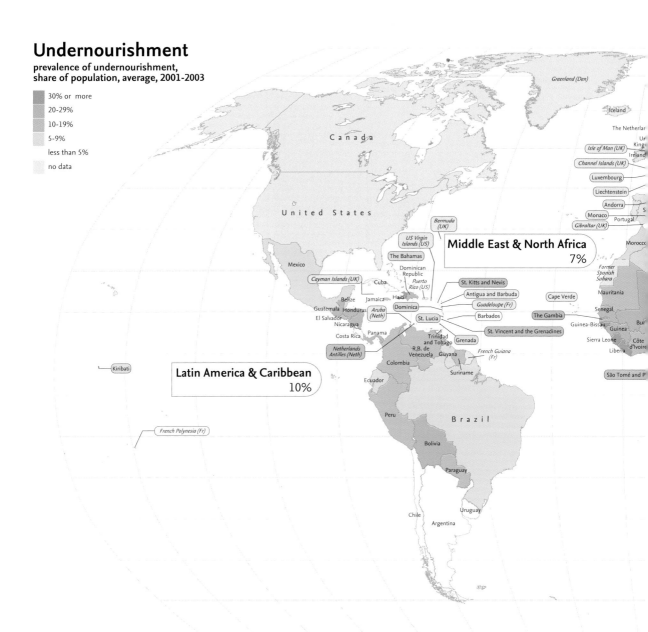

Greenland (Den)

Iceland

The Netherlar

Isle of Man (UK)
Channel Islands (UK)
Luxembourg
Liechtenstein
Andorra
Monaco
Gibraltar (UK)

Ur
King
Ireland

S

Portugal

Canada

United States

Middle East & North Africa
7%

Morocco

Former
Spanish
Sahara

Bermuda
(UK)

US Virgin
Islands (US)

The Bahamas

Mexico

Cayman Islands (UK)

Cuba

Dominican
Republic

Puerto
Rico (US)

Haiti

St. Kitts and Nevis
Antigua and Barbuda
Guadeloupe (Fr)

Cape Verde

Mauritania

Senegal

Belize
Jamaica
Guatemala Honduras
El Salvador
Nicaragua
Costa Rica

Dominica

Aruba
(Neth)

St. Lucia
Barbados
St. Vincent and the Grenadines

The Gambia

Guinea-Bissau Guinea

Bur

Panama

Trinidad
and Tobago
Grenada

Sierra Leone

Côte
d'Ivoire

Liberia

Netherlands
Antilles (Neth)

R.B. de
Venezuela

Guyana

French Guiana
(Fr)

Kiribati

Latin America & Caribbean
10%

Colombia

Suriname

São Tomé and P

Ecuador

Peru

B r a z i l

French Polynesia (Fr)

Bolivia

Paraguay

Chile

Uruguay

Argentina

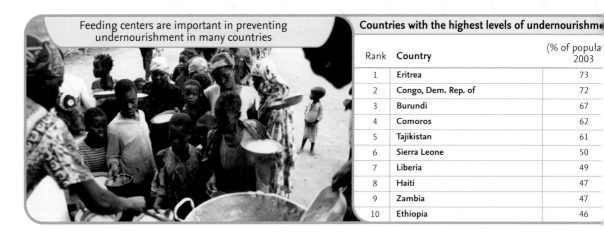

Feeding centers are important in preventing undernourishment in many countries

Countries with the highest levels of undernourishme

Rank	Country	(% of popula 2003
1	Eritrea	73
2	Congo, Dem. Rep. of	72
3	Burundi	67
4	Comoros	62
5	Tajikistan	61
6	Sierra Leone	50
7	Liberia	49
8	Haiti	47
9	Zambia	47
10	Ethiopia	46

Europe & Central Asia
6%

East Asia & Pacific
12%

South Asia
21%

Sub-Saharan Africa
32%

Facts	Internet links	
Among developing regions, only Latin America and the Caribbean has reduced the prevalence of hunger quickly enough since 1990 to reach the Millennium Development Goal target of halving hunger by 2015.	► Food and Agricultural Organization	**www.fao.org/faostat/ foodsecurity/index_en.htm**
Maternal mortality ratios are more than 10 times higher in countries where over 35 percent of the population is undernourished, compared with countries where less than 5 percent of the population is undernourished.	► World Bank	**www.worldbank.org**
The rural poor make up an estimated 80 percent of the world's 800 million hungry people	► WHO	**www.who.int/en/**
A large proportion of the hungry are concentrated in areas that are vulnerable to environmental degradation and climate change.	► World Food Programme	**www.wfp.org**
	► International Fund for Agricultural Development	**www.ifad.org**

Water is crucial to economic growth and development—and to the survival of both terrestrial and aquatic ecosystems. More than 670 million people live in countries facing chronic and widespread water shortages and more than a billion people lack access to safe drinking water.

Freshwater supplies are declining. With the projected growth in population and economic activity, the share of the world's population facing water shortages will increase more than fivefold by 2050. These trends pose a significant challenge for meeting the Millennium Development Goals and sustaining the growth of developing countries.

Although the earth's water resources are estimated at 1,400 million cubic kilometers, only a tiny fraction is usable for human needs. Freshwater is only 3 percent of total water resources, or about 44 million cubic kilometers. Most freshwater occurs in the form of permanent ice or snow, locked up in Antarctica and Greenland, or in deep groundwater aquifers. The principal sources of water for human use are lakes, rivers, soil moisture and relatively shallow groundwater basins. The usable portion of these sources is less than 1 percent of all freshwater and only 0.01 per cent of all water on earth, and much of that is located far from human populations.

South Asia and Middle East and North Africa face severe water scarcity

Freshwater resources per capita (thousand cubic meters) 2004

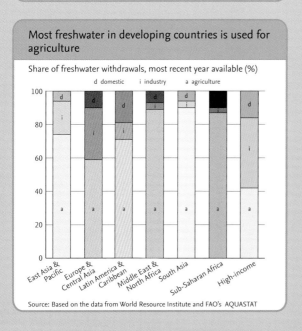

Source: Based on the data from World Resource Institute and FAO's AQUASTAT

Most freshwater in developing countries is used for agriculture

Share of freshwater withdrawals, most recent year available (%)

d domestic   i industry   a agriculture

Source: Based on the data from World Resource Institute and FAO's AQUASTAT

Irrigated lands are increasing, putting more pressure on water resources

Irrigated land (% of cropland)

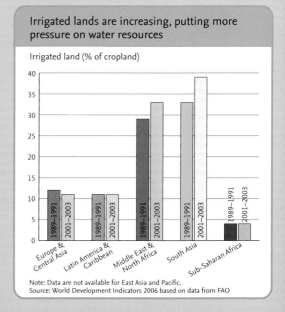

Note: Data are not available for East Asia and Pacific.
Source: World Development Indicators 2006 based on data from FAO

The diversion of water for irrigation has resulted in the Aral Sea shrinking, causing health problems and destroying the fishing industry

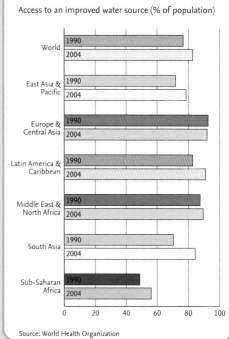

Despite progress, a large portion of the population in Sub-Saharan Africa does not have access to an improved water source

Access to an improved water source (% of population)

Source: World Health Organization

Humans compete with ecosystems in the use of freshwater. Extraction of water for human needs diminishes the total available to maintain the ecosystems' integrity. Pollution of water bodies leads to the further degradation of natural systems. The three major factors leading to increased water demand over the past century have been population growth, industrial development, and the expansion of irrigated agriculture. Agriculture accounts for more than 70 per cent of freshwater withdrawn from lakes, rivers, and underground sources. This share is about 88 percent in low-income countries. Most is used for irrigation, to provide about 40 percent of world food production.

Although domestic use of water for drinking and washing is the smallest source of demand, providing safe water for human consumption is of great importance for health and wellbeing. Water supplies should be free of chemical and biological contaminants and should be delivered in such a way that their cleanliness is protected and they are regularly and conveniently available. At present more than 1 billion people lack access to an adequately protected source of water within 1 kilometer of their dwelling, most of them in rural areas.

Access to improved water sources is a challenge particularly in rural areas

People without access to improved water (millions) 2004

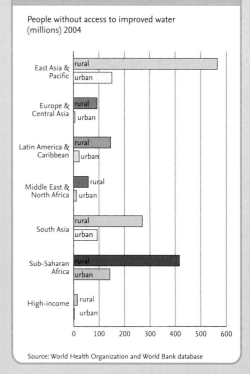

Source: World Health Organization and World Bank database

Freshwater

internal freshwater resources per capita
(cubic meters) 2004

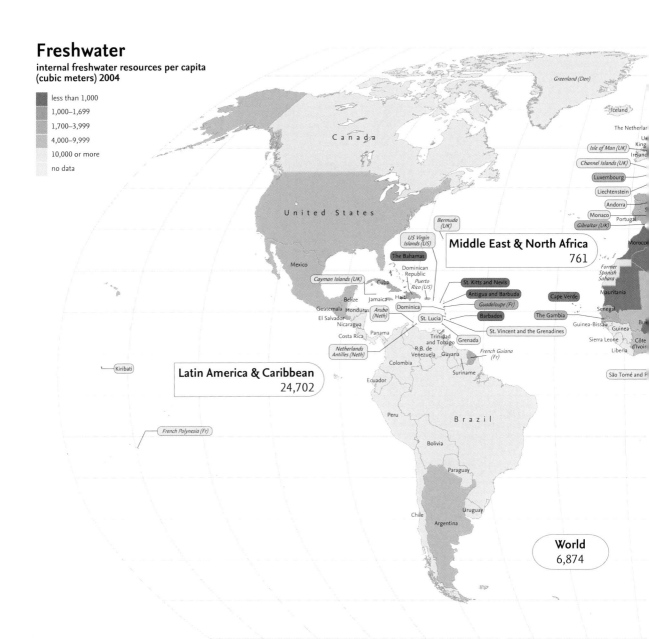

- less than 1,000
- 1,000–1,699
- 1,700–3,999
- 4,000–9,999
- 10,000 or more
- no data

Greenland (Den)

Iceland

The Netherlar

Isle of Man (UK)

Channel Islands (UK)

Luxembourg

Liechtenstein

Andorra

Monaco Portugal

Gibraltar (UK)

Canada

United States

Bermuda (UK)

US Virgin Islands (US)

The Bahamas

Dominican Republic

Puerto Rico (US)

Cayman Islands (UK) Cuba

Jamaica Haiti

Middle East & North Africa
761

Morocco

Former Spanish Sahara

Mauritania

Senegal

Cape Verde

St. Kitts and Nevis

Antigua and Barbuda

Guadeloupe (Fr)

Barbados

The Gambia

Guinea-Bissau Guinea

Mexico

Belize

Guatemala Honduras

El Salvador

Nicaragua

Costa Rica Panama

Aruba (Neth)

Dominica

St. Lucia

St. Vincent and the Grenadines

Grenada

Trinidad and Tobago

R.B. de Venezuela

Netherlands Antilles (Neth)

Colombia

Guyana

French Guiana (Fr)

Suriname

Sierra Leone Côte d'Ivoir

Liberia

São Tomé and P

Kiribati

Latin America & Caribbean
24,702

Ecuador

Peru

B r a z i l

French Polynesia (Fr)

Bolivia

Paraguay

Chile

Argentina

Uruguay

World
6,874

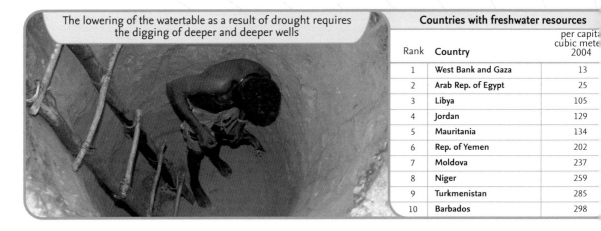

The lowering of the watertable as a result of drought requires the digging of deeper and deeper wells

Countries with freshwater resources

Rank	Country	per capita cubic meters 2004
1	West Bank and Gaza	13
2	Arab Rep. of Egypt	25
3	Libya	105
4	Jordan	129
5	Mauritania	134
6	Rep. of Yemen	202
7	Moldova	237
8	Niger	259
9	Turkmenistan	285
10	Barbados	298

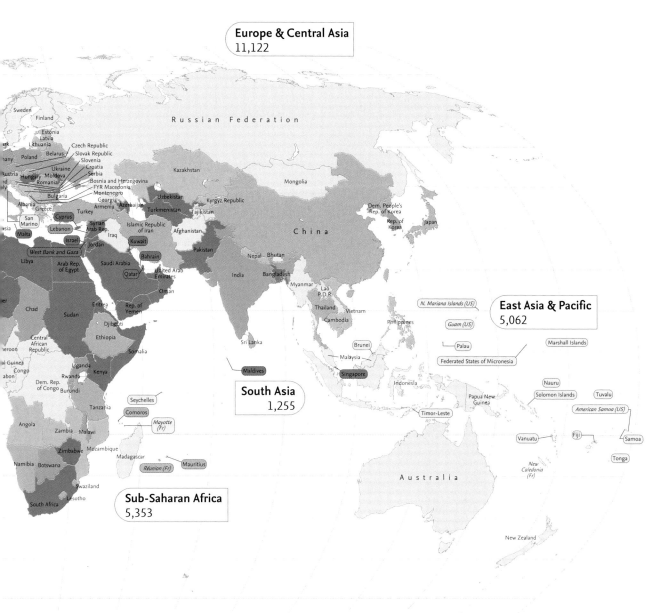

Europe & Central Asia
11,122

East Asia & Pacific
5,062

South Asia
1,255

Sub-Saharan Africa
5,353

Facts	Internet links	
The world's total volume of freshwater utilization has been over 3,800 billion cubic meters per year.	► AQUASTAT, Food and Agricultural Organization of the United Nations	**www.fao.org** click on 'statistical databases'
Agriculture uses 70 percent of freshwater globally.		
Latin America, with 31 percent, and Asia with 27 percent, have more than half of the world's freshwater resources.	► UN Environment Programme	**www.unep.org**
The Middle East and North Africa region has the lowest per capita freshwater resources: 760 cubic meters.		
By the year 2020 an estimated two-thirds of the world's population will be living in water-stressed countries – that is, less than 1,700 cubic meters per person per year.	► World Resource Institute	**www.wri.org**

Access to water

share of population with access to improved water source, 2004

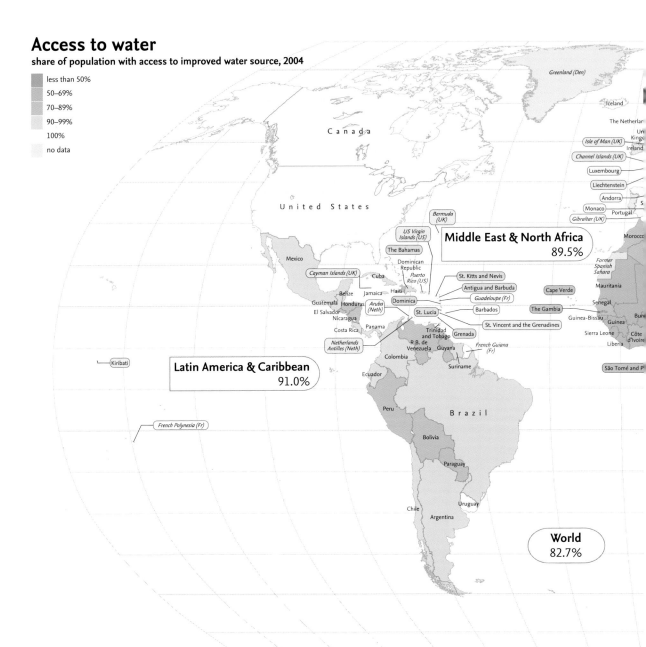

less than 50%
50–69%
70–89%
90–99%
100%
no data

Greenland (Den)

Iceland

The Netherlan

C a n a d a

Isle of Man (UK)
Channel Islands (UK)
Luxembourg
Liechtenstein
Andorra
Monaco
Gibraltar (UK)

Un
Kingc
Ireland

Portugal

United States

Bermuda (UK)

Middle East & North Africa
89.5%

Moroccc

US Virgin Islands (US)

The Bahamas

Former Spanish Sahara

Mexico

Cayman Islands (UK)
Cuba
Dominican Republic
Puerto Rico (US)

Mauritania

St. Kitts and Nevis
Antigua and Barbuda
Guadeloupe (Fr)
Barbados

Cape Verde

Senegal

Belize
Jamaica
Haiti

Guatemala Honduras
El Salvador
Nicaragua
Aruba (Neth)
Dominica
St. Lucia
St. Vincent and the Grenadines

The Gambia
Guinea-Bissau Guinea
Sierra Leone
Liberia

Bur
Côte d'Ivoire

Costa Rica Panama

Trinidad and Tobago Grenada
R.B. de Venezuela
Guyana

French Guiana (Fr)

São Tomé and P

Kiribati

Netherlands Antilles (Neth)

Colombia

Ecuador

Latin America & Caribbean
91.0%

Peru

B r a z i l

French Polynesia (Fr)

Bolivia

Paraguay

Chile
Uruguay
Argentina

World
82.7%

A standpipe such as this is often the only freshwater supply to communities in the developing world

Lowest access to an improved water source

Rank	Country	% of popula 2004
1	Ethiopia	22
2	Somalia	29
3	Afghanistan	39
4	Papua New Guinea	39
5	Cambodia	41
6	Chad	42
7	Equatorial Guinea	43
8	Mozambique	43
9	Madagascar	46
10	Niger	46

Europe & Central Asia
91.9%

East Asia & Pacific
78.5%

South Asia
84.4%

Sub-Saharan Africa
56.2%

Facts	Internet links	
Globally, around 1.1 billion people do not have access to improved water supply sources. Of those, 30 percent or about 322 million live in Sub-Saharan Africa.	▶ WHO/UNICEF Joint Monitoring Programme (JMP) for water supply and sanitation	www.wssinfo.org/en/welcome.html
In developing countries about 20 percent of the population do not have access to an improved source of water.	▶ WHO water, sanitation and health	www.who.int/water_sanitation_health/en
In Sub-Saharan Africa about 55 percent of the rural population do not have access to an improved source of water.		
The richest 20 percent of the households in developing countries are twice as likely to use drinking water from an improved source as the poorest.	▶ UNICEF ChildInfo	www.childinfo.org

Forests contribute to the livelihood of many of the one billion people living in extreme poverty. They nourish the natural systems supporting the agriculture and food supplies on which many more people depend. They also account for as much as 90 percent of terrestrial biodiversity. But in most countries they are shrinking.

Forests meet many people's basic, everyday needs, providing food, fuel, building materials, and clean water. Forests also provide essential public goods of global value: they facilitate the hydrological and nutrient cycles and act as carbon sinks, contributing to reduction of the greenhouse gases.

Forest loss is taking a terrible toll on both the natural and economic resources of many countries. Many of the world's rural poor directly depend on forest products for

Forests cover about 30 percent of all land

Forest coverage (% of land area) 1990–2005

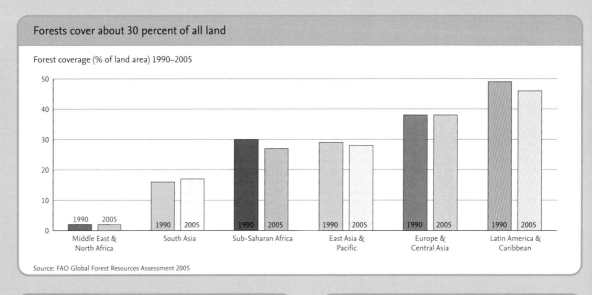

Source: FAO Global Forest Resources Assessment 2005

The largest forest losses have occurred in Sub-Saharan Africa and Latin America

Deforestation (million hectares) 1990–2005

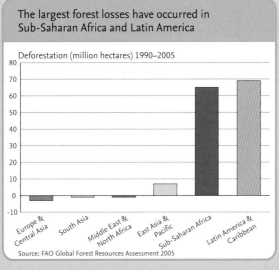

Source: FAO Global Forest Resources Assessment 2005

Protected areas conserve habitat for plants and animals

Nationally protected land area (% of land area) 2004

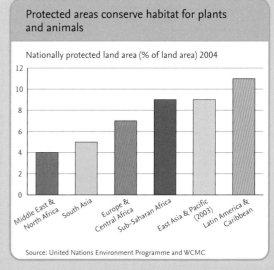

Source: United Nations Environment Programme and WCMC

Burned out forest in Amazonia, Para, Brazil

their livelihoods. In addition, deforestation is the main cause of biodiversity loss. Biodiversity refers to the variety of life on Earth, including the variety of plant and animal species, the genetic variability within each species, and the variety of different ecosystems. Tropical deforestation is a major source of the loss of ecosystems. In addition, forest loss in the tropics alone is responsible for 10–30 percent of global greenhouse gas emissions.

Deforestation is largely driven by economic development and human actions. For example, forests are cleared to expand agricultural land and timber is used to provide fuel and raw material for manufacturing and construction. Because many services provided by forests are not valued, they are subject to more destructive and unsustainable activities than is economically or environmentally justified.

In order to stop deforestation, incentives and regulations are key aspects of policy making. One of the most widely used approaches is to designate forests as protected areas. The total area of protected sites (both terrestrial and marine) has increased steadily in the past three decades. It is estimated that about 12 percent of the forest areas worldwide have been under protection. Designating land as protected, however, does not necessarily mean that protection is in force.

Rainforest protected from destruction within the Argentinian sector of Iguaçu National Park

Forest area

share of total land area, 2005

less than 10.0%
10.0–19.9%
20.0–29.9%
30.0–49.9%
50.0% or more
no data

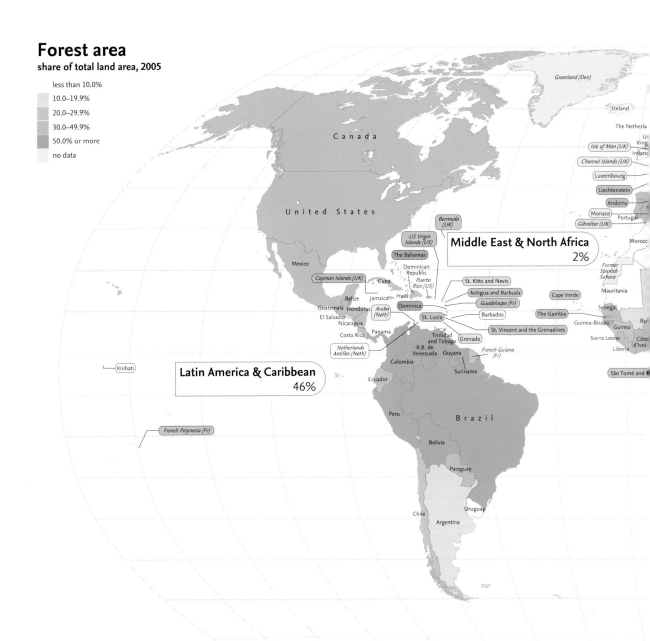

Greenland (Den)

Iceland

The Netherla

Isle of Man (UK)

Channel Islands (UK)

Luxembourg

Liechtenstein

Andorra

Monaco

Gibraltar (UK)

Portugal

C a n a d a

U n i t e d   S t a t e s

Bermuda (UK)

US Virgin Islands (US)

Middle East & North Africa
2%

Moroc

Mexico

The Bahamas

Dominican Republic

Cayman Islands (UK)

Cuba

Puerto Rico (US)

St. Kitts and Nevis

Antigua and Barbuda

Cape Verde

Former Spanish Sahara

Mauritania

Belize

Jamaica

Haiti

Dominica

Guadeloupe (Fr)

Senegal

Guatemala

Honduras

Aruba (Neth)

St. Lucia

Barbados

The Gambia

Guinea-Bissau

Bu

El Salvador

Nicaragua

Guinea

Costa Rica

Panama

St. Vincent and the Grenadines

Sierra Leone

Côte d'Ivoi

Netherlands Antilles (Neth)

Trinidad and Tobago

Grenada

R.B. de Venezuela

Guyana

French Guiana (Fr)

Liberia

Kiribati

Colombia

Suriname

São Tomé and

Latin America & Caribbean
46%

Ecuador

Peru

B r a z i l

French Polynesia (Fr)

Bolivia

Paraguay

Chile

Uruguay

Argentina

Virgin tropical rainforest, northern Brazil

Highest percentage of forest to land areas, 2

Rank	Country	Forest are % of land a
1	Suriname	95
2	Micronesia, Fed. Sts	90
3	American Samoa	90
4	Seychelles	87
5	Gabon	85
6	Solomon Islands	78
7	Guyana	77
8	Finland	74
9	Guinea-Bissau	74
10	Belize	72

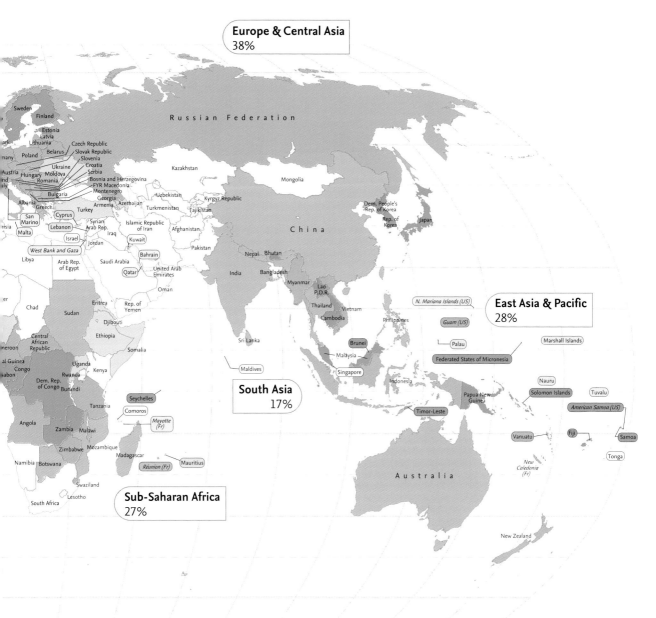

Europe & Central Asia
38%

East Asia & Pacific
28%

South Asia
17%

Sub-Saharan Africa
27%

Facts	Internet links	
The world's total forest area is about 3.9 billion hectares, which is roughly 30 percent of the total land area.	▶ United Nations Food and Agricultural Organization	**www.fao.org** (click on forestry)
Five countries, Russian Federation (20%), Brazil (12%), United States (8%), Canada (8%), and China (5%) contained more than half of the world's total forest area in 2005.	▶ United Nations Environment Programme and World Conservation and Monitoring Centre	**www.unep-wcmc.org**
China added about 4 million hectares of forest each year from 2000 to 2005.		
Europe and Central Asia has the highest level of forest area per capita—1.8 hectares. Latin America and the Caribbean is second with 1.6 hectares per capita.	▶ World Resources Institute	**www.wri.org** (click on research topics)

Forest lost and gained

average annual change in forest area, between 1990 and 2005

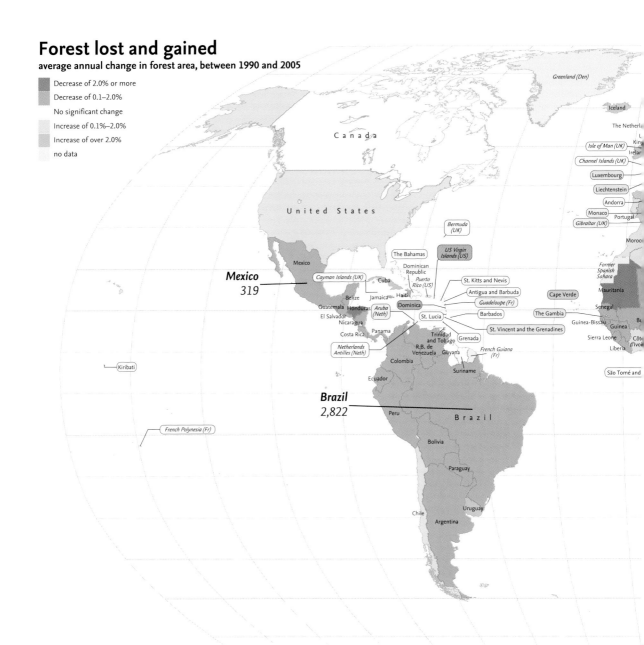

- ■ Decrease of 2.0% or more
- ■ Decrease of 0.1–2.0%
- No significant change
- Increase of 0.1%–2.0%
- Increase of over 2.0%
- no data

Mexico
319

Brazil
2,822

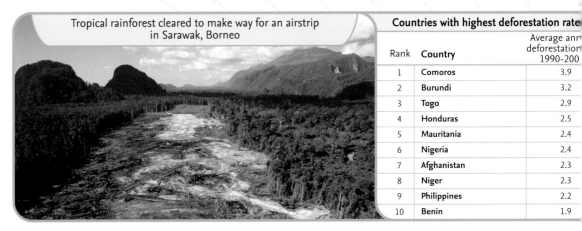

Tropical rainforest cleared to make way for an airstrip in Sarawak, Borneo

Countries with highest deforestation rate

Rank	Country	Average annual deforestation 1990-200
1	Comoros	3.9
2	Burundi	3.2
3	Togo	2.9
4	Honduras	2.5
5	Mauritania	2.4
6	Nigeria	2.4
7	Afghanistan	2.3
8	Niger	2.3
9	Philippines	2.2
10	Benin	1.9

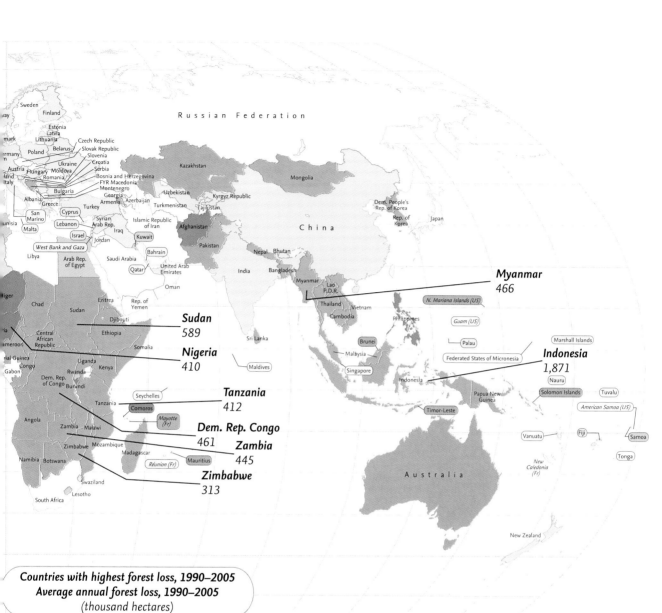

Myanmar
466

Sudan
589

Nigeria
410

Tanzania
412

Dem. Rep. Congo
461

Zambia
445

Zimbabwe
313

Indonesia
1,871

Countries with highest forest loss, 1990–2005
Average annual forest loss, 1990–2005
(thousand hectares)

Facts	Internet links	
Between 1990 and 2005, the world lost about 8 million hectares of forest each year or a total of 125 million hectares.	▶ United Nations Food and Agricultural Organization (FAO)	**www.fao.org** (click on forestry)
African forest area diminished by more than 65 million hectares, or about 50 percent of the world total forest loss, from 1990 to 2005.	▶ The World Conservation Union	**www.iucn.org**
Forest area in Brazil decreased by more than 15 million hectares, about 40 percent of the world total forest loss, between 2000 and 2005.	▶ World Wildlife Federation	**www.wwf.org**
At the global level, deforestation seems to be slowing; the estimate of forest cover change indicates an annual loss of 8.4 million hectares during the years 2000 to 2005, compared with 9.4 million hectares annually between 1990 and 2000.	▶ FAO's Global Forest Resources Assessment 2005	**www.fao.org/forestry**

Growing economies and expanding populations require more energy, most of which comes from fossil fuels. Burning fossil fuels and cutting forests have increased the levels of greenhouse gases in the atmosphere, changing the Earth's climate. Producing the energy needed for growth while mitigating global climate change is a challenge for everyone living on earth.

Developing countries use less than half of the world's energy, but their demand is growing faster than in the richer countries. In 2004, global energy consumption increased by 4.4 percent. In fast-growing East Asia and Pacific, consumption grew by 12.3 percent. As economies grow, two forces are at work: technological progress and a shift away from energy intensive activities, increasing energy efficiency. But rising incomes and growing populations increase the demand for energy. As a result, worldwide energy use increased by 30.5 percent between 1990 and 2004, compared to a population growth of only 21.1 percent.

Carbon dioxide (CO_2) emissions are highest in high-income economies, and still growing

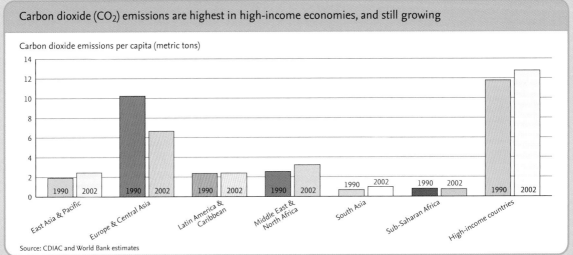

Carbon dioxide emissions per capita (metric tons)

Source: CDIAC and World Bank estimates

The five largest emitters account for more than half of all carbon dioxide produced each year, but average emissions per person in China and India are still quite low

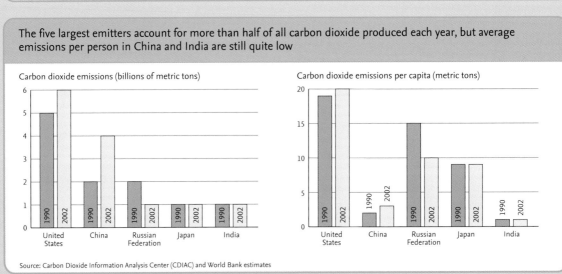

Carbon dioxide emissions (billions of metric tons)

Carbon dioxide emissions per capita (metric tons)

Source: Carbon Dioxide Information Analysis Center (CDIAC) and World Bank estimates

The way energy is generated determines the environmental damage done. The extensive use of fossil fuels in recent decades has boosted emission of carbon dioxide (CO_2), the principal greenhouse gas, which traps heat in the atmosphere. Burning coal releases twice as much carbon dioxide as burning the equivalent amount of natural gas. The amount of carbon released each year by human activities is estimated to be 6 to 7 billion tons. Some 2 billion tons are absorbed by oceans, and another 1.5 to 2.5 billion by plants, with the rest released in the atmosphere. Clearing of forests has decreased their ability to trap carbon dioxide.

The level of carbon dioxide in the atmosphere has increased by 30 percent since the beginning of the industrial revolution. According to the Intergovernmental Panel on Climate Change, the rate and duration of global warming in the 20th century are unprecedented in the past thousand years. The global average surface temperature has increased by about 0.6 degrees Celsius, with the 1990s being the warmest decade since 1861 when instrument records became available. Increases in the maximum temperature and the number of hot days have been observed over nearly all regions. And warming is expected to continue, with increases in the range of 1.4 to 5.8 degrees Celsius between 1990 and 2100.

Global warming shrinks glaciers, changes the frequency and intensity of rainfall, shifts growing seasons, advances the flowering of trees and emergence of insects, and causes the sea level to rise. The magnitude and effect of climate change vary across regions, but developing countries are likely to suffer most because of their dependence on climate-sensitive activities such as agriculture and fishing. They also have a more limited capacity to respond to the effects of climate change.

Deserts are advancing and rainfall is becoming less predictable as a result of global warming

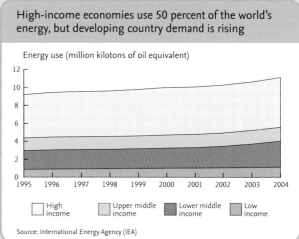

High-income economies use 50 percent of the world's energy, but developing country demand is rising

Energy use (million kilotons of oil equivalent)

High income / Upper middle income / Lower middle income / Low income

Source: International Energy Agency (IEA)

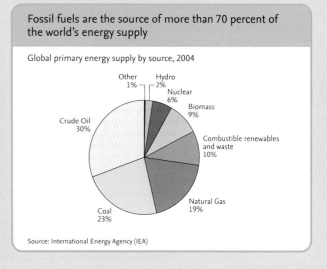

Fossil fuels are the source of more than 70 percent of the world's energy supply

Global primary energy supply by source, 2004

Other 1%
Hydro 2%
Nuclear 6%
Biomass 9%
Combustible renewables and waste 10%
Natural Gas 19%
Coal 23%
Crude Oil 30%

Source: International Energy Agency (IEA)

Energy use

**energy use per capita,
kilograms of oil equivalent, 2004**

- 5,000 or more
- 2,500-4,999
- 1,000-2,499
- 500-999
- less than 500
- no data

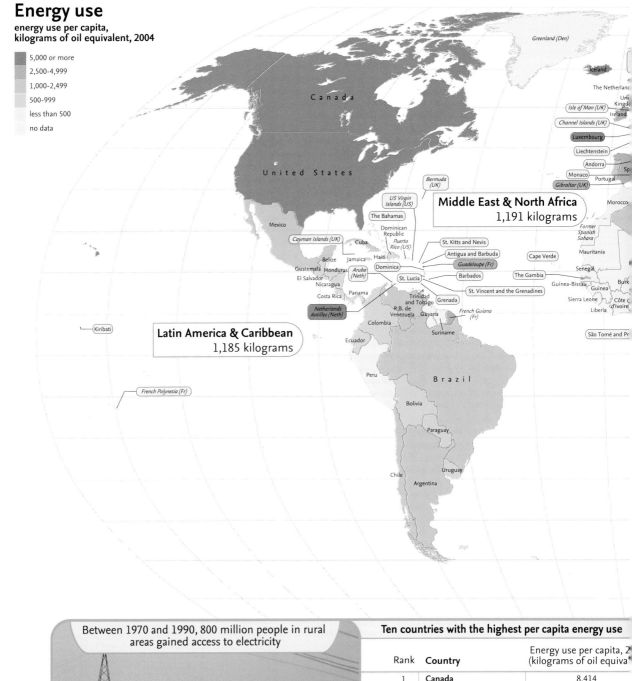

Greenland (Den)

Iceland

The Netherland

Isle of Man (UK)

Channel Islands (UK)

Luxembourg

Liechtenstein

Andorra

Monaco

Gibraltar (UK)

Uni
Kingdo
Ireland

Portugal

Sp

Canada

United States

Bermuda
(UK)

US Virgin
Islands (US)

The Bahamas

Mexico

Dominican
Republic

Morocco

Former
Spanish
Sahara

Middle East & North Africa
1,191 kilograms

Cayman Islands (UK)

Cuba

Puerto
Rico (US)

Mauritania

St. Kitts and Nevis

Antigua and Barbuda

Cape Verde

Belize

Jamaica

Haiti

Dominica

Guadeloupe (Fr)

Senegal

Guatemala Honduras

Aruba
(Neth)

Barbados

The Gambia

El Salvador

St. Lucia

Guinea-Bissau Guinea

Burk

Nicaragua

St. Vincent and the Grenadines

Costa Rica

Panama

Trinidad
and Tobago

Grenada

Sierra Leone

Côte
d'Ivoire

Netherlands
Antilles (Neth)

R.B. de
Venezuela

Guyana

French Guiana
(Fr)

Liberia

Colombia

Suriname

Kiribati

Latin America & Caribbean
1,185 kilograms

São Tomé and Pr

Ecuador

Peru

B r a z i l

French Polynesia (Fr)

Bolivia

Paraguay

Chile

Uruguay

Argentina

Between 1970 and 1990, 800 million people in rural areas gained access to electricity

Ten countries with the highest per capita energy use		
Rank	Country	Energy use per capita, 2 (kilograms of oil equiva
1	**Canada**	8,414
2	**United States**	7,920
3	**Finland**	7,286
4	**Singapore**	6,034
5	**Norway**	6,025
6	**Sweden**	5,998
7	**Australia**	5,757
8	**Belgium**	5,536
9	**Netherlands**	5,045
10	**France**	4,557

Europe & Central Asia
2,848 kilograms

East Asia & Pacific
1,124 kilograms

South Asia
486 kilograms

Sub-Saharan Africa
703 kilograms

Facts	Internet links	
High-income economies used 5.5 trillion metric tons of oil equivalent of energy in 2004, an amount equal to half of the world's total energy use.	▶ Intergovernmental Panel on Climate Change	www.ipcc.ch
In the developing world, more than 2 billion people do not have access to modern energy services and 2.4 billion people rely on traditional biomass for their basic energy needs. The indoor air pollution caused by the use of biomass in inefficient stoves is responsible for 1.5 million deaths per year—mostly of young children and mothers.	▶ International Energy Agency	www.iea.org
	▶ United Nations Statistics Division	www.unstats.un.org/unsd/energy
	▶ U.S. Energy Information Administration	www.eia.doe.gov
China, Canada, Brazil, and the United States produce about half of the world's hydropower energy.	▶ The World Bank Group Energy Program	www.worldbank.org/energy

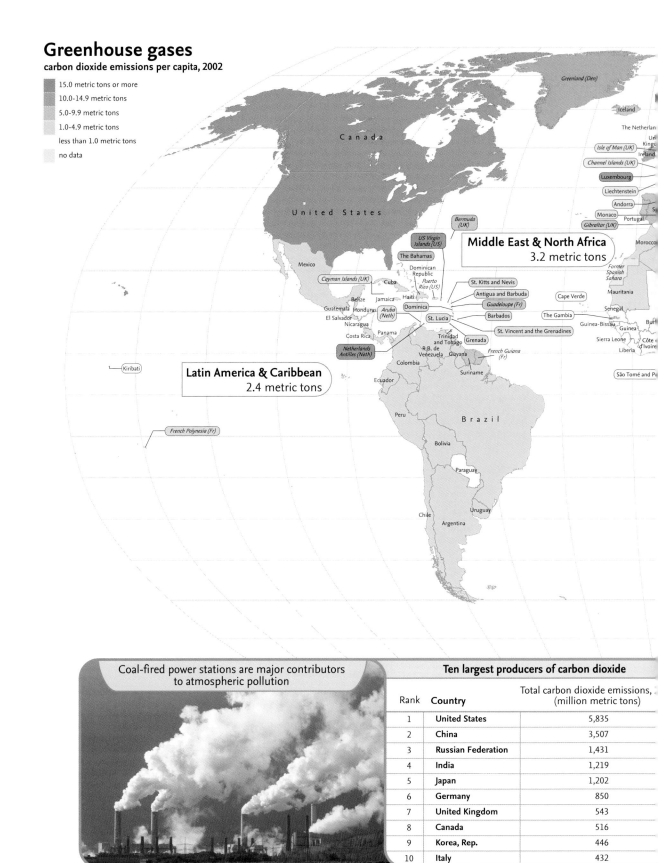

Greenhouse gases
carbon dioxide emissions per capita, 2002

- 15.0 metric tons or more
- 10.0-14.9 metric tons
- 5.0-9.9 metric tons
- 1.0-4.9 metric tons
- less than 1.0 metric tons
- no data

Middle East & North Africa
3.2 metric tons

Latin America & Caribbean
2.4 metric tons

Coal-fired power stations are major contributors to atmospheric pollution

Ten largest producers of carbon dioxide

Rank	Country	Total carbon dioxide emissions, (million metric tons)
1	United States	5,835
2	China	3,507
3	Russian Federation	1,431
4	India	1,219
5	Japan	1,202
6	Germany	850
7	United Kingdom	543
8	Canada	516
9	Korea, Rep.	446
10	Italy	432

Europe & Central Asia
6.7 metric tons

East Asia & Pacific
2.4 metric tons

South Asia
1.0 metric tons

Sub-Saharan Africa
0.7 metric tons

Facts	Internet links	
Between 1990 and 2002, the world's CO_2 emissions rose by almost 15 percent, to 24.4 billion metric tons.	▶ Intergovernmental Panel on Climate Change	**www.ipcc.ch**
The rapidly expanding economies of China and India are showing a swift increase in CO_2 emissions. China increased its emissions by 33 percent between 1992 and 2002, while India's emissions grew by 57 percent in the same period.	▶ Carbon Dioxide Information Analysis Center (CDIAC)	**cdiac.ornl.gov/home.html**
Europe and Central Asia cut CO_2 emissions from 10 metric tons per capita in 1990 to 6 in 2002 but still remains highest among developing regions.	▶ World Resource Institute	**climate.wri.org**
As well as contributing to global warming, regional climate changes, and accelerated sea-level rise, atmospheric CO_2 directly affects plant photosynthesis and water use, potentially altering vegetation and ecosystems.	▶ World Bank Prototype Carbon Fund	**www.prototypecarbonfund.org**

Economy	Total population millions 2005	Life expectancy at birth years 2004	Under-five mortality rate per 1,000 2004	Access to an improved water source % of population 2004	Gross national income (GNI)[a] $ billions 2005	per capita $ 2005
Afghanistan	..	..	..	39	7.0	.. c
Albania	3.1	74	19	96	8.1	2,580
Algeria	32.9	71	40	85	89.6	2,730
American Samoa	0.1	..	..	..	..	.. d
Andorra	0.1	..	7	100	..	.. e
Angola	15.9	41	260	53	21.5	1,350
Antigua and Barbuda	0.1	75	12	91	0.9	10,920
Argentina	38.7	75	18	96	173.0	4,470
Armenia	3.0	71	32	92	4.4	1,470
Aruba	0.1	..	..	100	..	.. e
Australia	20.3	80	6	100	654.6	32,220
Austria	8.2	79	5	100	303.6	36,980
Azerbaijan	8.4	72	90	77	10.4	1,240
Bahamas, The	0.3	70	13	97	..	..
Bahrain	0.7	75	11	..	10.3	14,370
Bangladesh	141.8	63	77	74	66.2	470
Barbados	0.3	75	12	100	..	.. d
Belarus	9.8	68	11	100	27.0	2,760
Belgium	10.5	79	5	100	373.8	35,700
Belize	0.3	72	39	91	1.0	3,500
Benin	8.4	55	152	67	4.3	510
Bermuda	0.1	78	..	..	..	.. e
Bhutan	0.9	64	80	62	0.8	870
Bolivia	9.2	65	69	85	9.3	1,010
Bosnia and Herzegovina	3.9	74	15	97	9.5	2,440
Botswana	1.8	35	116	95	9.1	5,180
Brazil	186.4	71	34	90	644.1	3,460
Brunei Darussalam	0.4	77	9	..	..	.. e
Bulgaria	7.7	72	15	99	26.7	3,450
Burkina Faso	13.2	48	192	61	5.2	400
Burundi	7.5	44	190	79	0.7	100
Cambodia	14.1	57	141	41	5.3	380
Cameroon	16.3	46	149	66	16.5	1,010
Canada	32.3	80	6	100	1,051.9	32,600
Cape Verde	0.5	70	36	80	0.9	1,870
Cayman Islands	0.0	..	..	..	..	.. e
Central African Republic	4.0	39	193	75	1.4	350
Chad	9.7	44	200	42	3.9	400
Channel Islands	0.1	79	..	..	..	.. e
Chile	16.3	78	8	95	95.7	5,870
China	1,304.5	71	31	77	2,263.8	1,740
Hong Kong, China	6.9	82	..	..	192.1	27,670
Macao, China	0.5	80	..	..	..	.. e
Colombia	45.6	73	21	93	104.5	2,290
Comoros	0.6	63	70	86	0.4	640
Congo, Dem. Rep. of	57.5	44	205	46	6.9	120
Congo, Rep.	4.0	52	108	58	3.8	950
Costa Rica	4.3	79	13	97	19.9	4,590
Côte d'Ivoire	18.2	46	194	84	15.3	840
Croatia	4.4	75	7	100	35.8	8,060
Cuba	11.3	77	7	91	..	.. f
Cyprus	0.8	79	5	100	13.6	16,510
Czech Republic	10.2	76	4	100	109.2	10,710
Denmark	5.4	77	5	100	256.8	47,390
Djibouti	0.8	53	126	73	0.8	1,020
Dominica	0.1	77	14	97	0.3	3,790
Dominican Republic	8.9	68	32	95	21.1	2,370
Ecuador	13.2	75	26	94	34.8	2,630
Egypt, Arab Rep. of	74.0	70	36	98	92.9	1,250
El Salvador	6.9	71	28	84	16.8	2,450
Equatorial Guinea	0.5	43	204	43	..	.. d
Eritrea	4.4	54	82	60	1.0	220
Estonia	1.3	72	8	100	12.2	9,100
Ethiopia	71.3	42	166	22	11.1	160
Faeroe Islands	0.0	..	..	..	..	.. e
Fiji	0.8	68	20	47	2.8 g	3,280
Finland	5.2	79	4	100	196.5	37,460
France	60.7	80	5	100	2,177.7	34,810 g
French Polynesia	0.3	74	..	100	..	..
Gabon	1.4	54	91	88	6.9	5,010
Gambia, The	1.5	56	122	82	0.4	290
Georgia	4.5	71	45	82	6.0	1,350
Germany	82.5	78	5	100	2,852.3	34,580
Ghana	22.1	57	112	75	10.0	450
Greece	11.1	79	5	..	218.1	19,670
Greenland	0.1	69	..	..	..	.. e
Grenada	0.1	73	21	95	0.4	3,920
Guam	0.2	75	..	100	..	.. e
Guatemala	12.6	68	45	95	30.3	2,400

Total debt service % of exports of goods, services and income 2004	Merchandise trade % of GDP 2005	Foreign direct investment net inflows, % of GDP 2004	Starting a business time required in days April 2006	Fixed-line and mobile phone subscribers[b] per 1,000 people 2004	Carbon dioxide emissions per capita metric tons 2002	Economy
..	52.5	..	8	23	..	Afghanistan
2.6	39.4	5.7	39	154	0.8	Albania
..	63.0	1.0	24	215	2.9	Algeria
..	..	..	..	..	..	American Samoa
..	..	..	..	..	..	Andorra
14.8	111.5	7.4	124	54	0.5	Angola
..	73.7	..	21	1,149	4.7	Antigua and Barbuda
28.5	37.5	2.7	32	579	3.5	Argentina
8.0	55.4	6.1	24	260	1.0	Armenia
..	50.7	16.0	..	..	..	Aruba
..	33.0	6.7	2	1,359	18.1	Australia
..	81.5	1.4	29	1,438	7.9	Austria
5.2	68.1	41.0	53	333	3.4	Azerbaijan
..	39.7	3.5	..	1,023	6.7	Bahamas, The
..	135.9	..	..	1,175	30.6	Bahrain
5.2	38.5	0.8	37	37	0.3	Bangladesh
5.2	63.0	1.8	..	1,249	4.6	Barbados
2.1	110.6	0.7	69	578	6.0	Belarus
..	178.2	11.4	27	1,333	8.9	Belgium
62.5	87.7	12.3	45	465	3.0	Belize
7.6	36.9	1.5	31	38	0.3	Benin
..	..	..	..	1,337	7.7	Bermuda
..	77.3	0.1	62	53	0.5	Bhutan
18.6	52.2	1.3	50	269	1.2	Bolivia
3.7	102.9	7.2	54	507	4.7	Bosnia and Herzegovina
1.2	88.7	0.5	108	396	2.3	Botswana
46.8	24.7	3.0	152	587	1.8	Brazil
..	..	..	..	660	17.7	Brunei Darussalam
17.1	112.2	8.3	32	966	5.3	Bulgaria
11.9	32.3	0.7	34	37	0.1	Burkina Faso
66.0	48.8	0.5	43	12	0.0	Burundi
0.8	126.1	2.7	86	40	0.0	Cambodia
..	29.1	0.0	37	103	0.2	Cameroon
..	60.9	0.6	3	1,053	16.5	Canada
5.3	44.7	2.2	52	281	0.3	Cape Verde
..	..	..	..	..	..	Cayman Islands
..	22.3	-1.0	14	18	0.1	Central African Republic
..	74.6	11.1	75	14	0.0	Chad
..	..	..	..	..	..	Channel Islands
24.2	62.5	8.0	27	799	3.6	Chile
3.5	63.8	2.8	35	499	2.7	China
..	333.6	20.5	11	1,733	5.2	Hong Kong, China
..	71.6	..	..	1,326	4.0	Macao, China
33.0	34.7	3.2	44	427	1.3	Colombia
..	24.9	0.5	23	26	0.1	Comoros
..	64.0	2.8	155	37	0.0	Congo, Dem. Rep. of
4.0	137.1	5.6	71	102	0.6	Congo, Rep.
7.3	86.6	3.4	77	533	1.4	Costa Rica
6.9	73.9	1.1	45	98	0.4	Côte d'Ivoire
27.2	73.1	3.6	45	1,065	4.7	Croatia
..	..	..	..	75	2.1	Cuba
..	41.8	7.2	..	1,282	8.3	Cyprus
10.5	127.0	4.1	24	1,392	11.2	Czech Republic
..	63.8	-3.6	5	1,599	8.8	Denmark
..	53.0	5.0	37	43	0.5	Djibouti
9.7	73.8	6.8	19	879	1.7	Dominica
6.4	53.2	3.5	73	396	2.5	Dominican Republic
36.0	53.6	3.5	65	472	2.0	Ecuador
7.6	30.1	1.6	19	235	2.1	Egypt, Arab Rep. of
8.8	59.5	2.9	26	402	1.0	El Salvador
..	278.6	51.4	136	106	0.4	Equatorial Guinea
3.1	51.1	3.2	76	14	0.2	Eritrea
15.7	134.6	9.3	35	1,260	11.7	Estonia
5.3	44.9	5.6	16	8	0.1	Ethiopia
..	..	..	..	1,224	..	Faeroe Islands
..	84.0	-0.4	46	254	1.6	Fiji
..	64.6	1.7	14	1,407	12.0	Finland
..	45.3	1.2	8	1,299	6.2	France
..	34.6	..	..	586	2.9	French Polynesia
10.9	75.1	4.5	60	388	2.6	Gabon
..	53.4	15.0	27	99	0.2	Gambia, The
11.2	52.5	9.7	16	337	0.7	Georgia
..	62.7	-1.3	24	1,525	10.3	Germany
6.6	71.2	1.6	81	93	0.4	Ghana
..	33.3	0.7	38	1,465	8.5	Greece
..	..	..	..	800	10.0	Greenland
15.9	86.3	9.7	52	719	2.2	Grenada
..	..	..	..	713	25.4	Guam
7.4	38.8	0.6	30	350	0.9	Guatemala

Economy	Total population millions 2005	Life expectancy at birth years 2004	Under-five mortality rate per 1,000 2004	Access to an improved water source % of population 2004	Gross national income (GNI)[a] $ billions 2005	per capita $ 2005
Guinea	9.4	54	155	50	3.5	370
Guinea-Bissau	1.6	45	203	59	0.3	180
Guyana	0.8	64	64	83	0.8	1,010
Haiti	8.5	52	117	54	3.9	450
Honduras	7.2	68	41	87	8.6	1,190
Hungary	10.1	73	8	99	101.2	10,030
Iceland	0.3	80	3	100	13.7	46,320
India	1,094.6	63	85	86	793.0	720
Indonesia	220.6	67	38	77	282.2	1,280
Iran, Islamic Rep. of	67.7	71	38	94	187.4	2,770
Iraq	..	..	..	81	..	.. f
Ireland	4.2	78	6	..	166.6	40,150
Isle of Man	0.1	78	..	..	2.1	27,770
Israel	6.9	79	6	100	128.7	18,620
Italy	57.5	80	5	..	1,724.9	30,010
Jamaica	2.7	71	20	93	9.0	3,400
Japan	128.0	82	4	100	4,988.2	38,980
Jordan	5.4	72	27	97	13.5	2,500
Kazakhstan	15.1	65	73	86	44.4	2,930
Kenya	34.3	48	120	61	18.0	530
Kiribati	0.1	63	65	65	0.1	1,390
Korea, Dem. Rep.	22.5	64	55	100	..	.. c
Korea, Rep. of	48.3	77	6	92	764.7	15,830
Kuwait	2.5	77	12	..	59.1	24,040
Kyrgyz Republic	5.2	68	68	77	2.3	440
Lao P.D.R.	5.9	55	83	51	2.6	440
Latvia	2.3	71	12	99	15.5	6,760
Lebanon	3.6	72	31	100	22.1	6,180
Lesotho	1.8	36	112	79	1.7	960
Liberia	3.3	42	235	61	0.4	130
Libya	5.9	74	20	..	32.4	5,530
Liechtenstein	0.0	..	5	..	..	.. e
Lithuania	3.4	72	8	..	24.1	7,050
Luxembourg	0.5	78	6	100	30.0	65,630
Macedonia, FYR	2.0	74	14	..	5.8	2,830
Madagascar	18.6	56	123	46	5.4	290
Malawi	12.9	40	175	73	2.1	160
Malaysia	25.3	73	12	99	125.8	4,960
Maldives	0.3	67	46	83	0.8	2,390
Mali	13.5	48	219	50	5.1	380
Malta	0.4	79	6	100	5.5	13,590
Marshall Islands	0.1	65	59	87	0.2	2,930
Mauritania	3.1	53	125	53	1.7	560
Mauritius	1.2	73	15	100	6.6	5,260
Mayotte	0.2	..	..	..	..	.. d
Mexico	103.1	75	28	97	753.4	7,310
Micronesia, Fed. Sts. of	0.1	68	23	94	0.3	2,300
Moldova	4.2	68	28	92	3.2 h	880 h
Monaco	0.0	..	5	100	..	.. e
Mongolia	2.6	65	52	62	1.8	690
Morocco	30.2	70	43	81	52.3	1,730
Mozambique	19.8	42	152	43	6.1	310
Myanmar	50.5	61	106	78	..	.. c
Namibia	2.0	47	63	87	6.1	2,990
Nepal	27.1	62	76	90	7.3	270
Netherlands	16.3	79	6	100	598.0	36,620
Netherlands Antilles	0.2	76	..	..	..	.. e
New Caledonia	0.2	75	..	..	..	.. e
New Zealand	4.1	79	7	..	106.7	25,960
Nicaragua	5.5	70	38	79	5.0	910
Niger	14.0	45	259	46	3.3	240
Nigeria	131.5	44	197	48	74.2	560
Northern Mariana Islands	0.1	..	..	99	..	.. d
Norway	4.6	80	4	100	275.2	59,590
Oman	2.6	75	13	..	23.0	9,070
Pakistan	155.8	65	101	91	107.3	690
Palau	0.0	..	27	85	0.2	7,630
Panama	3.2	75	24	90	15.0	4,630
Papua New Guinea	5.9	56	93	39	3.9	660
Paraguay	6.2	71	24	86	7.9	1,280
Peru	28.0	70	29	83	73.0	2,610
Philippines	83.1	71	34	85	108.3	1,300
Poland	38.2	74	8	..	271.4	7,110
Portugal	10.6	77	5	..	170.7	16,170
Puerto Rico	3.9	77	..	..	..	.. e
Qatar	0.8	74	21	100	..	.. e
Romania	21.6	71	20	57	82.9	3,830
Russian Federation	143.2	65	21	97	639.1	4,460
Rwanda	9.0	44	203	74	2.1	230

Total debt service % of exports of goods, services and income 2004	Merchandise trade % of GDP 2005	Foreign direct investment net inflows, % of GDP 2004	Starting a business time required in days April 2006	Fixed-line and mobile phone subscribers[b] per 1,000 people 2004	Carbon dioxide emissions per capita metric tons 2002	Economy
19.9	65.3	2.6	49	15	0.1	Guinea
16.1	66.4	1.9	233	8	0.2	Guinea-Bissau
5.8	177.5	3.8	46	329	2.2	Guyana
4.0	45.8	0.2	203	64	0.2	Haiti
7.8	77.5	4.0	44	153	0.9	Honduras
25.2	117.2	4.6	38	1,217	5.6	Hungary
..	53.6	2.5	5	1,650	7.7	Iceland
18.9	28.2	0.8	35	85	1.2	India
22.1	54.0	0.4	97	184	1.4	Indonesia
10.7	50.9	0.3	47	270	5.5	Iran, Islamic Rep. of
..	155.9	..	77	57	..	Iraq
..	89.6	6.1	19	1,425	11.0	Ireland
..	..	..	..	..	..	Isle of Man
..	72.5	1.4	34	1,499	10.6	Israel
..	43.3	1.0	13	1,541	7.5	Italy
14.8	62.4	6.8	8	1,021	4.1	Jamaica
..	24.7	0.2	23	1,176	9.4	Japan
8.2	114.6	5.4	18	419	3.3	Jordan
38.0	80.6	9.5	20	350	9.9	Kazakhstan
8.6	54.6	0.3	54	85	0.2	Kenya
..	73.3	..	21	52	0.3	Kiribati
..	..	..	..	41	6.5	Korea, Dem. Rep.
..	69.3	1.2	22	1,303	9.4	Korea, Rep. of
..	82.3	0.0	35	1,015	25.6	Kuwait
14.2	72.9	3.5	21	106	1.0	Kyrgyz Republic
9.0	36.4	0.7	163	48	0.2	Lao P.D.R.
21.1	87.2	5.1	16	937	2.7	Latvia
..	50.5	1.3	46	429	4.7	Lebanon
4.5	143.5	9.0	73	109	..	Lesotho
..	250.7	4.0	..	3	0.1	Liberia
..	97.0	..	..	156	9.1	Libya
..	..	..	..	1,338	..	Liechtenstein
14.3	107.0	3.4	26	1,235	3.6	Lithuania
..	115.1	246.9	..	1,998	21.3	Luxembourg
10.5	91.4	2.9	18	642	5.1	Macedonia, FYR
6.0	45.6	1.0	21	19	0.1	Madagascar
7.6	72.2	0.8	37	25	0.1	Malawi
7.9	196.4	3.9	30	766	6.3	Malaysia
4.6	110.5	1.8	13	451	3.4	Maldives
5.8	52.0	3.7	42	36	0.0	Mali
..	105.5	..	..	1,249	7.4	Malta
..	103.2	..	17	86	..	Marshall Islands
..	60.9	19.6	82	135	1.1	Mauritania
7.4	82.4	0.2	46	700	2.6	Mauritius
..	..	..	..	..	..	Mayotte
22.9	58.0	2.5	27	554	3.8	Mexico
..	62.5	..	16	226	..	Micronesia, Fed. Sts. of
12.1	117.1	3.1	30	391	1.6	Moldova
..	..	..	..	..	..	Monaco
2.9	116.5	5.8	20	184	3.4	Mongolia
14.0	59.1	1.5	12	357	1.5	Morocco
4.5	63.5	4.1	113	27	0.1	Mozambique
3.8	..	..	..	10	0.2	Myanmar
..	72.5	..	95	206	1.1	Namibia
5.5	36.6	0.3	31	22	0.2	Nepal
..	127.6	0.1	10	1,393	9.3	Netherlands
..	..	..	..	..	27.8	Netherlands Antilles
..	57.0	..	..	738	8.2	New Caledonia
..	44.0	2.3	12	1,189	8.6	New Zealand
5.8	70.3	5.6	39	177	0.7	Nicaragua
7.5	39.1	0.5	24	13	0.1	Niger
8.2	59.3	2.6	43	79	0.4	Nigeria
..	..	..	..	..	..	Northern Mariana Islands
..	55.7	0.2	13	1,530	13.9	Norway
6.9	91.4	-0.1	34	413	12.1	Oman
21.2	37.3	1.2	24	63	0.7	Pakistan
..	..	..	28	..	..	Palau
14.3	34.0	7.1	19	388	2.0	Panama
12.7	101.0	0.6	56	19	0.4	Papua New Guinea
13.5	53.7	1.3	74	344	0.7	Paraguay
17.1	37.9	2.6	72	223	1.0	Peru
20.9	89.0	0.5	48	446	0.9	Philippines
34.6	63.3	5.0	31	777	7.7	Poland
..	56.6	0.5	8	1,384	6.0	Portugal
..	..	..	7	974	3.5	Puerto Rico
..	86.8	..	..	877	53.0	Qatar
17.2	69.2	7.2	11	673	4.0	Romania
9.8	48.5	2.1	28	508	9.8	Russian Federation
11.2	24.9	0.4	16	18	0.1	Rwanda

Economy	Total population millions 2005	Life expectancy at birth years 2004	Under-five mortality rate per 1,000 2004	Access to an improved water source % of population 2004	Gross national income (GNI)[a] $ billions 2005	Gross national income (GNI)[a] per capita $ 2005
Samoa	0.2	70	30	88	0.4	2,090
San Marino	0.0	..	4	..	0.7	.. e
São Tomé and Príncipe	0.2	63	118	79	0.1	390
Saudi Arabia	24.6	72	27	..	289.2	11,770
Senegal	11.7	56	137	76	8.2	710
*Serbia and Montenegro	8.2 i	73	15	93	26.8 i	3,280 i
Seychelles	0.1	73	14	88	0.7	8,290
Sierra Leone	5.5	41	283	57	1.2	220
Singapore	4.4	79	3	100	119.6	27,490
Slovak Republic	5.4	74	9	100	42.8	7,950
Slovenia	2.0	77	4	..	34.7	17,350
Solomon Islands	0.5	63	56	70	0.3	590
Somalia	8.2	47	225	29	..	.. c
South Africa	45.2	45	67	88	224.1	4,960
Spain	43.4	80	5	100	1,100.1	25,360
Sri Lanka	19.6	74	14	79	22.8	1,160
St. Kitts and Nevis	0.0	71	..	99	0.4	8,210
St. Lucia	0.2	73	14	98	0.8	4,800
St. Vincent and the Grenadines	0.1	71	22	..	0.4	3,590
Sudan	36.2	57	91	70	23.3	640
Suriname	0.4	69	39	92	1.1	2,540
Swaziland	1.1	42	156	62	2.6	2,280
Sweden	9.0	80	4	100	370.5	41,060
Switzerland	7.4	81	5	100	408.7	54,930
Syrian Arab Republic	19.0	74	16	93	26.3	1,380
Tajikistan	6.5	64	93	59	2.2	330
Tanzania	38.3	46	126	62	12.7 k	340 k
Thailand	64.2	71	21	99	176.9	2,750
Timor-Leste	1.0	..	80	58	0.7	750
Togo	6.1	55	140	52	2.2	350
Tonga	0.1	72	25	100	0.2	2,190
Trinidad and Tobago	1.3	70	20	91	13.6	10,440
Tunisia	10.0	73	25	93	29.0	2,890
Turkey	72.6	70	32	96	342.2	4,710
Turkmenistan	4.8	63	103	72	..	.. f
Uganda	28.8	49	138	60	7.9	280
Ukraine	47.1	68	18	96	71.4	1,520
United Arab Emirates	4.5	79	8	100	102.7	23,770
United Kingdom	60.2	79	6	100	2,263.7	37,600
United States	296.5	77	8	100	12,969.6	43,740
Uruguay	3.5	75	17	100	15.1	4,360
Uzbekistan	26.6	67	69	82	13.5	510
Vanuatu	0.2	69	40	60	0.3	1,600
Venezuela, R.B. de	26.6	74	19	83	127.8	4,810
Vietnam	83.0	70	23	85	51.7	620
Virgin Islands (U.S.)	0.1	79	..	..	..	.. e
West Bank and Gaza	3.6	73	..	92	3.8	1,120
Yemen, Rep. of	21.0	61	111	67	12.7	600
Zambia	11.7	38	182	58	5.7	490
Zimbabwe	13.0	37	129	81	4.5	340
World	6,437.8 s	67 w	79 w	83 w	44,983.3 t	6,987 w
Low income	2,353.0	59	122	75	1,363.9	580
Middle income	3,073.5	70	39	84	8,113.1	2,640
Lower middle income	2,474.7	70	42	82	4,746.5	1,918
Upper middle income	598.7	69	28	94	3,367.9	5,625
Low and middle income	5,426.4	65	86	80	9,476.8	1,746
East Asia & Pacific	1,885.3	70	37	79	3,067.4	1,627
Europe & Central Asia	472.9	69	34	92	1,945.0	4,113
Latin America & the Caribbean	551.4	72	31	91	2,209.7	4,008
Middle East & North Africa	305.4	69	55	89	684.6	2,241
South Asia	1,470.0	63	92	84	1,005.3	684
Sub-Saharan Africa	741.4	46	168	56	552.2	745
High income	1,011.3	79	7	100	35,528.8	35,131
European Monetary Union	310.6	79	5	100	9,912.4	31,914

See page 142 for explanation of symbols.

Notes: Numbers in *italics* are for years other than those specified.

a. Calculated using the *World Bank Atlas* method.

b. Data are from the International Telecommunication Union's *World Telecommunication Development Report* database and World Bank estimates.

c. Estimated to be low income ($875 or less).

d. Estimated to be upper middle income ($3,466–$10,725).

e. Estimated to be high income ($10,726 or more).

Total debt service % of exports of goods, services and income 2004	Merchandise trade % of GDP 2005	Foreign direct investment net inflows, % of GDP 2004	Starting a business time required in days April 2006	Fixed-line and mobile phone subscribers[b] per 1,000 people 2004	Carbon dioxide emissions per capita metric tons 2002	Economy
..	51.8	0.2	35	130	0.8	Samoa
..	..	..	..	1,342	..	San Marino
25.6	94.1	94.5	144	79	0.6	São Tomé and Príncipe
..	75.8	..	39	537	15.0	Saudi Arabia
10.3	59.3	0.9	58	72	0.4	Senegal
..	61.7	4.0	18 j	910	..	Serbia and Montenegro
8.1	136.2	5.3	38	842	6.4	Seychelles
10.9	41.9	2.4	26	27	0.1	Sierra Leone
..	368.0	14.9	6	1,350	13.7	Singapore
13.8	144.9	2.7	25	1,027	6.8	Slovak Republic
..	114.1	2.5	60	1,278	7.7	Slovenia
..	85.1	-1.9	57	17	0.4	Solomon Islands
..	..	..	..	88	..	Somalia
6.4	49.3	0.3	35	473	7.6	South Africa
..	41.3	1.6	47	1,321	7.4	Spain
8.5	65.0	1.2	50	165	0.5	Sri Lanka
24.5	70.6	15.5	47	745	2.4	St. Kitts and Nevis
7.9	81.2	14.6	40	411	2.4	St. Lucia
7.3	84.3	13.8	12	642	1.6	St. Vincent and the Grenadines
6.0	40.6	7.0	39	58	0.3	Sudan
..	136.1	..	694	659	5.1	Suriname
1.7	150.3	2.7	61	119	0.9	Swaziland
..	67.9	-0.2	16	1,743	5.8	Sweden
..	67.5	-0.2	20	1,560	5.6	Switzerland
3.5	52.3	1.1	43	269	2.8	Syrian Arab Republic
6.8	96.3	13.1	67	46	0.7	Tajikistan
5.3	34.2	2.2	30	32	0.1	Tanzania
10.6	129.3	0.9	33	537	3.7	Thailand
..	..	..	92	..	..	Timor-Leste
2.0	81.9	2.9	53	48	0.3	Togo
2.5	50.3	0.0	32	144	1.0	Tonga
3.8	91.6	8.1	43	745	31.8	Trinidad and Tobago
13.7	82.5	2.1	11	480	2.3	Tunisia
35.9	52.2	0.9	9	751	3.0	Turkey
..	125.8	..	..	82	9.1	Turkmenistan
6.9	30.8	3.3	30	44	0.1	Uganda
10.7	86.2	2.6	33	545	6.4	Ukraine
..	138.5	..	63	1,128	25.0	United Arab Emirates
..	40.1	3.4	18	1,584	9.2	United Kingdom
..	21.2	0.9	5	1,223	20.2	United States
34.9	40.8	2.4	43	465	1.2	Uruguay
..	61.1	1.2	29	79	4.8	Uzbekistan
1.4	52.9	6.9	39	83	0.4	Vanuatu
16.0	58.4	1.4	141	450	4.3	Venezuela, R.B. de
6.0	131.9	3.6	50	131	0.8	Vietnam
..	..	..	..	1,010	92.8	Virgin Islands (U.S.)
..	..	..	93	380	..	West Bank and Gaza
3.5	63.7	1.1	63	92	0.7	Yemen, Rep. of
20.2	61.6	6.2	35	34	0.2	Zambia
..	110.3	1.3	96	55	1.0	Zimbabwe
.. w	47.1 w	1.6 w	48 u	471 w	3.9 w	World
10.1	41.1	1.4	59	71	0.8	Low income
15.0	62.2	2.7	51	482	3.3	Middle income
13.1	58.8	2.6	57	431	2.6	Lower middle income
17.0	66.7	2.9	42	563	6.2	Upper middle income
14.5	59.3	2.5	54	307	2.2	Low and middle income
6.8	74.7	2.5	46	431	2.4	East Asia & Pacific
19.6	68.7	3.5	32	536	6.7	Europe & Central Asia
26.4	44.0	3.0	73	499	2.4	Latin America & the Caribbean
10.6	57.0	1.1	41	219	3.2	Middle East & North Africa
12.4	31.0	0.8	33	76	1.0	South Asia
7.9	58.8	2.2	62	84	0.7	Sub-Saharan Africa
..	43.6	1.4	21	1,309	12.8	High income
..	61.9	1.7	22	1,430	8.3	European Monetary Union

f. Estimated to be lower middle income ($876–$3,465).
g. Data include the French overseas departments of French Guiana, Guadeloupe, Martinique, and Réunion.
h. Excludes data for Transnistria.
i. Excludes data for Kosovo.
j. Data refer to Serbia only. Corresponding figure for Montenegro is 24 days.
k. Data refer to mainland Tanzania only.

*Following a referendum in May 2006, Montenegro declared its independence from the union of Serbia and Montenegro, resulting in both states becoming independent countries. Data are for both states prior to independence.

Rank	Country	$
1	Luxembourg	65,630
2	Norway	59,590
3	Switzerland	54,930
4	Bermuda	.. a
5	Denmark	47,390
6	Iceland	46,320
7	United States	43,740
8	Liechtenstein	.. a
9	Sweden	41,060
10	Ireland	40,150
11	Japan	38,980
12	United Kingdom	37,600
13	Finland	37,460
14	Channel Islands	.. a
15	Austria	36,980
16	Netherlands	36,620
17	Belgium	35,700
18	France	34,810 b
19	Germany	34,580
20	Canada	32,600
21	Australia	32,220
22	Isle of Man	27,770 c
26	Italy	30,010
28	Hong Kong, China	27,670
29	Singapore	27,490
31	New Zealand	25,960
32	Kuwait	24,040 c
33	Spain	25,360
34	United Arab Emirates	23,770 c
38	Greece	19,670
41	Israel	18,620
44	Cyprus	16,510 c
46	Slovenia	17,350
48	Portugal	16,170
49	Korea, Rep. of	15,830
50	Bahrain	14,370 c
53	Malta	13,590
55	Saudi Arabia	11,770
56	Antigua and Barbuda	10,920
57	Czech Republic	10,710
58	Trinidad and Tobago	10,440
60	Hungary	10,030
62	Oman	9,070 c
63	Estonia	9,100
65	Seychelles	8,290
66	St. Kitts and Nevis	8,210
67	Croatia	8,060
68	Slovak Republic	7,950
70	Palau	7,630
71	Mexico	7,310
72	Poland	7,110
73	Lithuania	7,050
74	Latvia	6,760
75	Lebanon	6,180
76	Chile	5,870
77	Libya	5,530
78	Mauritius	5,260
80	Botswana	5,180
81	Gabon	5,010
82	Malaysia	4,960
82	South Africa	4,960

Rank	Country	$
84	Venezuela, R.B. de	4,810
85	St. Lucia	4,800
86	Turkey	4,710
87	Panama	4,630
88	Costa Rica	4,590
89	Argentina	4,470
90	Russian Federation	4,460
91	Uruguay	4,360
92	Grenada	3,920
93	Romania	3,830
94	Dominica	3,790
95	St. Vincent and the Grenadines	3,590
96	Belize	3,500
97	Brazil	3,460
98	Bulgaria	3,450
99	Jamaica	3,400
100	Fiji	3,280
100	Serbia and Montenegro	3,280 d
102	Namibia	2,990
103	Kazakhstan	2,930
103	Marshall Islands	2,930
105	Tunisia	2,890
106	Macedonia, FYR	2,830
107	Iran, Islamic Rep. of	2,770
108	Belarus	2,760
109	Thailand	2,750
110	Algeria	2,730
112	Ecuador	2,630
113	Peru	2,610
114	Albania	2,580
115	Suriname	2,540
116	Jordan	2,500
117	El Salvador	2,450
118	Bosnia and Herzegovina	2,440
119	Guatemala	2,400
120	Maldives	2,390
121	Dominican Republic	2,370
122	Micronesia, Fed. Sts. of	2,300
123	Colombia	2,290
124	Swaziland	2,280
125	Tonga	2,190
126	Samoa	2,090
127	Cape Verde	1,870
128	China	1,740
129	Morocco	1,730
130	Vanuatu	1,600
131	Ukraine	1,520
132	Armenia	1,470
134	Kiribati	1,390
135	Syrian Arab Republic	1,380
136	Angola	1,350
136	Georgia	1,350
138	Philippines	1,300
139	Indonesia	1,280
139	Paraguay	1,280
139	West Bank and Gaza	1,120 c
142	Egypt, Arab Rep. of	1,250
143	Azerbaijan	1,240
144	Honduras	1,190
145	Sri Lanka	1,160
146	Djibouti	1,020

Rank	Country	$
147	Bolivia	1,010
147	Cameroon	1,010
147	Guyana	1,010
150	Lesotho	960
151	Congo, Rep.	950
152	Nicaragua	910
153	Moldova	880 e
155	Bhutan	870
156	Côte d'Ivoire	840
158	Timor-Leste	750
159	India	720
160	Senegal	710
161	Mongolia	690
161	Pakistan	690
163	Papua New Guinea	660
164	Comoros	640
164	Sudan	640
166	Vietnam	620
167	Yemen, Rep. of	600
168	Solomon Islands	590
169	Mauritania	560
169	Nigeria	560
171	Kenya	530
172	Benin	510
172	Uzbekistan	510
174	Zambia	490
175	Bangladesh	470
176	Ghana	450
176	Haiti	450
178	Kyrgyz Republic	440
178	Lao P.D.R.	440
180	Burkina Faso	400
180	Chad	400
182	São Tomé and Príncipe	390
183	Cambodia	380
183	Mali	380
185	Guinea	370
186	Central African Republic	350
186	Togo	350
188	Tanzania	340 f
188	Zimbabwe	340
190	Tajikistan	330
191	Mozambique	310
192	Gambia, The	290
192	Madagascar	290
194	Uganda	280
195	Nepal	270
196	Niger	240
197	Rwanda	230
199	Eritrea	220
199	Sierra Leone	220
201	Guinea-Bissau	180
202	Ethiopia	160
202	Malawi	160
206	Liberia	130
207	Congo, Dem. Rep. of	120
208	Burundi	100

Note: Rankings include all 208 economies presented in the key indicators table, but only those that have confirmed World Bank Atlas GNI per capita estimates or rank in the top twenty are shown.

Estimated ranges for economies that do not have confirmed World Bank Atlas GNI per capita figures are:

High income ($10,726 and above):
Andorra
Aruba
Bahamas, The
Brunei Darussalam
Cayman Islands
Faeroe Islands
French Polynesia
Greenland
Guam
Macao, China
Monaco
Netherlands Antilles
New Caledonia
Puerto Rico
Qatar
San Marino
Virgin Islands (U.S.)

Upper middle income ($3,466 – $10,725):
American Samoa
Barbados
Equatorial Guinea
Mayotte
Northern Mariana Islands

Lower middle income ($876 – $3,465):
Cuba
Iraq
Turkmenistan

Low income ($875 or less):
Afghanistan
Korea, Dem. Rep. of
Myanmar
Somalia

a. Data not available; ranking is approximate.
b. Data include the French overseas departments of French Guiana, Guadeloupe, Martinique, and Réunion.
c. Data are for earlier year; ranking is approximate.
d. Data exclude Kosovo.
e. Data exclude Transnistria.
f. Data refer to mainland Tanzania only.

Following a referendum in May 2006, Montenegro declared its independence from the union of Serbia and Montenegro, resulting in both states becoming independent countries. Data are for both states prior to independence.

The need for statistics

This book would not be possible without the efforts of statisticians, who conduct surveys, collect data, and compile statistics to produce estimates of the indicators shown here. Although statisticians rarely hit the headlines, the statistics they produce often do. The growth of the economy, the rate of unemployment, the prevalence of diseases—these and many other statistical indicators regularly make the front pages in countries around the world.

Most of the statistics included here are produced by governments or other public authorities. They describe the social and economic conditions of people, how they have changed over time, and how they compare to other countries. They are shared through a network of international agencies which work together to assemble a global database that describes the state of the world. Published and distributed in many forms, they are used by governments, the private sector, and non-governmental organizations to guide their decision making.

Statistics make the detailed analysis of complex social and economic problems possible, helping policy makers to choose the best interventions and then to monitor the results. Rates of poverty, economic growth, mortality, literacy, and employment, are all affected by the actions of governments. Good quality statistics, produced by professionals using sound methods and reliable data, and free from political interference, provide information to citizens about the successes and failures of public policy. Good statistics promote debate about the best policy choices.

When the United Nations met in September 2000 to set goals for the new millennium, the goals for social and economic development were defined by specific, quantifiable, time-bound targets—reducing poverty by half, ensuring all children complete primary school, achieving gender equality in education, reducing child mortality rates by two thirds, cutting maternal mortality rates by three quarters, and increasing access to safe water and sanitation, all by 2015. These are ambitious goals. They are intended to draw public attention to the need for faster progress and firm commitments to achieving development results. Reliable statistics are needed to monitor progress and encourage greater effort.

The use of statistics for improving the lives of people is not new. Well over a century ago, Charles Booth produced detailed maps illustrating wellbeing and social class differences in London, using data gathered over a period of 20 years. These maps informed a famous policy debate which contributed to the development of radically new programs aimed at the alleviation of poverty in London. Earlier in the 19th century, John Snow, a London doctor, discovered a statistical pattern among cholera cases which led to the removal of a pump that was the source of contamination of a water supply.

Statistics are a public good. Once they have been produced, they can be used for many purposes. For instance, most countries compile statistics from surveys of prices paid by consumers, which are in turn used to estimate rates of price inflation. These statistics have widespread uses, but two in particular are familiar to many people: rates of inflation often figure in wage and salary negotiations and are used for pension adjustments. And financial markets monitor inflation to gauge the strength of demand or anticipate changes in monetary policy.

The example of prices is interesting, because statistics are also used to set prices. Take the case of agricultural products. Harvest sizes are estimated by governments from sample surveys of farms. These production statistics help market operators assess levels of supply, which wholesalers and retailers compare to demand for those products during the price bargaining process. Thus, public statistics make private markets more efficient.

Although statistics are vitally important for efficiently allocating scarce resources, in many of the world's poorest countries the statistics produced by governments are of poor quality. In over 50 countries, policymakers don't know how many people live in poverty, and in over 100 countries they can't determine whether the number is shrinking or growing.

In very poor countries the administrative systems that produce official statistics are fragile. Record-keeping is not always given high priority in places where governments lack resources and struggle to provide the most basic services. Surveys and censuses are carried out irregularly. And the professional statisticians, who manage statistical processes and provide the technical know-how needed to produce good quality statistics, are often underpaid and in short supply. When statistics are unreliable, policymakers cannot make use of them in their decision making, leading to poor decisions and poor outcomes.

Recent innovations have helped improve statistics at relatively low cost. Combining the extensive information collected on households from sample surveys with the finer spatial disaggregation obtained from population censuses provides a method of estimating poverty levels for small areas. Combined with information about the location of public facilities, this technique has been very useful for policy makers and program managers, because it helps them identify vulnerable and underserved populations. It does not require additional data collection activities because it combines existing sources. Providing researchers with access to survey and census datasets, under controlled conditions to protect the confidentiality of survey respondents, is another way in which some countries have expanded the use of statistics. Electronic dissemination tools have dramatically reduced the costs of publishing statistical data and have enabled them to reach a far wider audience.

The international community increasingly recognizes the role that good data and statistics play in development, and the importance of encouraging their use. There is a global effort underway to improve the capacity of developing countries to produce and analyze statistical data. The key aim is to improve the data for monitoring progress towards the Millennium Development Goals. A sustained effort will be needed to put statistical capacity at the center of development policy, to increase investment in data collection, dissemination, and technical capacity, and to improve the use of existing datasets.

Millennium Development Goals

Goals and targets from the Millennium Declaration	Indicators for monitoring progress

Goal 1   Eradicate extreme poverty and hunger

Target 1   Halve, between 1990 and 2015, the proportion of people whose income is less than one dollar a day

1. Proportion of population below $1 (PPP) per day[a]
1a. Poverty headcount ratio (percentage of population below the national poverty line)
2. Poverty gap ratio (incidence x depth of poverty)
3. Share of poorest quintile in national consumption

Target 2   Halve, between 1990 and 2015, the proportion of people who suffer from hunger

4. Prevalence of underweight children under five years of age
5. Proportion of population below minimum level of dietary energy consumption

Goal 2   Achieve universal primary education

Target 3   Ensure that, by 2015, children everywhere, boys and girls alike, will be able to complete a full course of primary schooling

6. Net enrollment ratio in primary education
7. Proportion of pupils starting grade 1 who reach grade 5[b]
8. Literacy rate of 15–24-year-olds

Goal 3   Promote gender equality and empower women

Target 4   Eliminate gender disparity in primary and secondary education, preferably by 2005, and in all levels of education no later than 2015

9. Ratio of girls to boys in primary, secondary, and tertiary education
10. Ratio of literate women to men, ages 15–24 years
11. Share of women in wage employment in the non-agricultural sector
12. Proportion of seats held by women in national parliament

Goal 4   Reduce child mortality

Target 5   Reduce by two-thirds, between 1990 and 2015, the under-5 mortality rate

13. Under-five mortality rate
14. Infant mortality rate
15. Proportion of one-year-old children immunized against measles

Goals and targets from the Millennium Declaration	Indicators for monitoring progress

Goal 5 Improve maternal health

Target 6 Reduce by three-quarters, between 1990 and 2015, the maternal mortality ratio	16. Maternal mortality ratio 17. Proportion of births attended by skilled health personnel

Goal 6 Combat HIV/AIDS, malaria and other diseases

Target 7 Have halted by 2015, and begun to reverse, the spread of HIV/AIDS	18. HIV prevalence among pregnant women ages 15–24 years 19. Condom use rate of the contraceptive prevalence rate[c] 19a. Condom use at last high-risk sex 19b. Percentage of population ages 15–24 years with comprehensive correct knowledge of HIV/AIDS[d] 19c. Contraceptive prevalence rate 20. Ratio of school attendance of orphans to school attendance of non-orphans ages 10–14 years
Target 8 Have halted by 2015, and begun to reverse, the incidence of malaria and other major diseases	21. Prevalence and death rates associated with malaria 22. Proportion of population in malaria-risk areas using effective malaria prevention and treatment measures[e] 23. Prevalence and death rates associated with tuberculosis 24. Proportion of tuberculosis cases detected and cured under directly observed treatment, short course (DOTS)

Goal 7 Ensure environmental sustainability

Target 9 Integrate the principles of sustainable development into country policies and programs and reverse the loss of environmental resources	25. Proportion of land area covered by forest 26. Ratio of area protected to maintain biological diversity to surface area 27. Energy use (kilograms of oil equivalent) per $1 GDP (PPP) 28. Carbon dioxide emissions per capita and consumption of ozone-depleting chlorofluorocarbons (ODP tons) 29. Proportion of population using solid fuels
Target 10 Halve, by 2015, the proportion of people without sustainable access to safe drinking water and basic sanitation	30. Proportion of population with sustainable access to an improved water source, urban and rural 31. Proportion of population with access to improved sanitation, urban and rural
Target 11 By 2020, to have achieved a significant improvement in the lives of at least 100 million slum dwellers	32. Proportion of households with access to secure tenure

Millennium Development Goals

Goals and targets from the Millennium Declaration	Indicators for monitoring progress

Goal 8 Develop a global partnership for development

Target 12 Develop further an open, rule-based, predictable, non-discriminatory trading and financial system.

Includes a commitment to good governance, development and poverty reduction—both nationally and internationally

Target 13 Address the special needs of the least developed countries

Includes: tariff- and quota-free access for the least developedcountries' exports; enhanced programme of debt relief for heavily indebted poor countries (HIPC) and cancellation of official bilateral debt; and more generous ODA for countries committed to poverty reduction

Target 14 Address the special needs of landlocked countries and small island developing states (through the Programme of Action for the Sustainable Development of Small Island Developing States and the outcome of the 22nd special session of the General Assembly)

Target 15 Deal comprehensively with the debt problems of developing countries through national and international measures in order to make debt sustainable in the long term

Some of the indicators listed below are monitored separately for the least developed countries (LDCs), Africa, landlocked countries and small island developing states.

Official Development Assistance

33. Net ODA, total and to the least developed countries, as a percentage of OECD/DAC donors' gross national income

34. Proportion of total bilateral, sector-allocable ODA of OECD/DAC donors to basic social services (basic education, primary health care, nutrition, safe water and sanitation)

35. Proportion of bilateral official development assistance of OECD/DAC donors that is untied

36. ODA received in landlocked countries as a proportion of their gross national incomes

37. ODA received in small island developing states as proportion of their gross national incomes

Market access

38. Proportion of total developed country imports (by value and excluding arms) from developing countries and from the least-developed countries, admitted free of duty

39. Average tariffs imposed by developed countries on agricultural products and textiles and clothing from developing countries

40. Agricultural support estimate for OECD countries as a percentage of their gross domestic product

41. Proportion of ODA provided to help build trade capacity

Debt sustainability

42. Total number of countries that have reached their HIPC decision points and number that have reached their HIPC completion points (cumulative)

43. Debt relief committed under HIPC Initiative

44. Debt service as a percentage of exports of goods and services

Target 16 In cooperation with developing countries, develop and implement strategies for decent and productive work for youth

45. Unemployment rate of young people ages 15–24 years, each sex and total[f]

Target 17 In cooperation with pharmaceutical companies, provide access to affordable essential drugs in developing countries

46. Proportion of population with access to affordable essential drugs on a sustainable basis

Target 18 In cooperation with the private sector, make available the benefits of new technologies, especially information and communications

47. Telephone lines and cellular subscribers per 100 people

48a. Personal computers in use per 100 people

48b. Internet users per 100 people

Note: Goals, targets, and indicators effective 8 September 2003.

[a]For monitoring country poverty trends, indicators based on national poverty lines should be used, where available.

[b]An alternative indicator under development is 'primary completion rate'.

[c]Among contraceptive methods, only condoms are effective in preventing HIV transmission. Since the condom use rate is only measured among women in union, it is supplemented by an indicator on condom use in high-risk situations (Indicator 19a) and an indicator on HIV/AIDS knowledge (Indicator 19b). Indicator 19c (contraceptive prevalence rate) is also useful in tracking progress in other health, gender, and poverty goals.

[d]This indicator is defined as the percentage of 15- to 24-year-olds who correctly identify the two major ways of preventing the sexual transmission of HIV (using condoms and limiting sex to one faithful, uninfected partner), who reject the two most common local misconceptions about HIV transmission, and who know that a healthy-looking person can transmit HIV. However, since there are currently an insufficient number of surveys to be able to calculate the indicator as defined above, UNICEF, in collaboration with UNAIDS and WHO, produced two proxy indicators that represent two components of the actual indicator. They are:

- the percentage of women and men ages 15–24 who know that a person can protect him/herself from HIV infection by 'consistent use of condom'; and
- the percentage of women and men ages 15–24 who know a healthy-looking person can transmit HIV.

[e]Prevention to be measured by the percentage of children under age five sleeping under insecticide-treated bednets; treatment to be measured by percentage of children under age five who are appropriately treated.

[f]An improved measure of the target for future years is under development by the International Labour Organization.

Definitions, sources, notes, and abbreviations

Access to an all-season road The number of rural people who live within 2 km (typically equivalent to a 20-minute walk) of an all-season road. An 'all-season road' is a road that is motorable all year by the prevailing means of rural transport. Predictable interruptions of short duration during inclement weather (e.g. heavy rainfall) are accepted, particularly on low-volume roads. (World Bank)

Adolescent fertility rate The number of births per 1000 women aged 15–19. (United Nations Population Division)

Agricultural machinery Wheel and crawler tractors (excluding garden tractors) in use in agriculture. (FAO)

Agricultural productivity The ratio of agricultural value added, measured in constant 2000 US dollars, to the number of workers in agriculture. (FAO)

Agricultural products Plant and animal products, including tree crops but excluding timber and fish products. (FAO)

Agriculture The output of the agricultural sector corresponds to International Standard Industrial Classification (ISIC) divisions 1–5 (includes hunting, forestry, and fishing).

Aid dependency ratios Net official aid and official development assistance, each expressed as a share of GNI aid per capita provide a measure of the recipient country's dependency on aid. Calculated using values in US dollars converted at official exchange rates. (OECD)

Aid, net Aid flows classified as official development assistance or official aid, net of repayments. (OECD)

Births attended by skilled health staff The proportion of deliveries attended by personnel trained to give the necessary supervision, care, and advice to women during pregnancy, labor, and the postpartum period, to conduct deliveries on their own, and to care for newborns. (UNICEF)

Business, number of procedures to start up The number of procedures required to start a business, including interactions required to obtain necessary permits and licenses and to complete all inscriptions, verifications, and notifications to start operations. Data are for businesses with specific characteristics of ownership, size, and type, and type of production. (World Bank).

Business, time to start up The time, in calendar days, needed to complete all the procedures required to legally operate a business. If a procedure can be speeded up at additional cost, the fastest procedure, regardless of cost, is chosen. Time spent gathering information about the registration process is excluded. (World Bank)

Carbon dioxide emissions Emissions stemming from the burning of fossil fuels (including the consumption of solid, liquid, and gas fuels and gas flaring) and the manufacture of cement. (Carbon Dioxide Information Analysis Center)

Cereal yield The production of wheat, rice, maize, barley, oats, rye, millet, sorghum, buckwheat, and mixed grains, measured in kilograms per hectare of harvested land. Refers to crops harvested for dry grain only. (FAO)

Children out of school, primary school age children The number of primary school age children not enrolled in primary or secondary school. (UNESCO Institute for Statistics)

Children with acute respiratory infection taken to a health provider The proportion of children under age five with acute respiratory infection in the two weeks prior to the survey who were taken to an appropriate health provider. (UNICEF)

Control of corruption Measures the perceptions of corruption, conventionally defined as the exercise of public power for private gain. (World Bank)

Crop production index Agricultural production for each period relative to the base period 1989–91. It includes all crops except fodder crops. (FAO)

Crude birth and death rates Number of births and deaths that occur during the year, per

1,000 population, estimated at mid-year.

Debt, total external Debt owed to nonresidents repayable in foreign currency, goods, or services. It is the sum of public, publicly guaranteed, and private nonguaranteed long-term debt, use of IMF credit, and short-term debt. Short-term debt includes all debt having an original maturity of one year or less and interest in arrears on long-term debt. (World Bank)

Debt service, total The sum of principal repayments and interest actually paid in foreign currency, goods, or services on long-term debt, interest paid on short-term debt; and repayments (repurchases and charges) to the International Monetary Fund.
(World Bank)

Deforestation The permanent conversion of natural forest area to other uses, including shifting cultivation, permanent agriculture, ranching, settlements, and infrastructure development. Deforested areas do not include areas logged but intended for regeneration or areas degraded by fuelwood gathering, acid precipitation, or forest fires. Negative numbers indicate an increase in forest area. (FAO)

Dependency ratio The ratio of dependents— people younger than 15 and older than 64— to the working-age population. (World Bank)

Education, primary The level of education that provides children with basic reading, writing, and mathematics skills along with an elementary understanding of such subjects as history, geography, natural science, social science, art, and music.
(UNESCO Institute for Statistics)

Education, secondary The level of education that completes the provision of basic education. It is aimed at laying the foundations for lifelong learning and human development by offering more subject- or skill-oriented instruction using more specialized teachers.
(UNESCO Institute for Statistics)

Education, tertiary The level of education, whether or not leading to an advanced research qualification, that normally requires, as a minimum condition of

admission, the successful completion of education at the secondary level.
(UNESCO Institute for Statistics)

Electric power consumption The output of power plants and combined heat and power plants minus transmission, distribution, and transformation losses and own use by heat and power plants. (IEA)

Energy use, commercial The apparent consumption of commercial energy equals domestic production plus imports and stock changes, minus exports and fuels supplied to ships and aircraft engaged in international transport. (IEA)

Enrollment rate, gross The ratio of children who are enrolled in an education level, regardless of age, to the population of the corresponding official school age, as defined by the International Standard Classification of Education 1997 (ISCED97).
(UNESCO Institute for Statistics)

Enrollment rate, net The ratio of children of official school age, as defined by the International Standard Classification of Education 1997 (ISCED97), who are enrolled in school, to the population of the corresponding official school age.
(UNESCO Institute for Statistics)

Exchange rate, official The exchange rate (local currency units relative to the US dollar) determined by national authorities or the rate determined in the legally sanctioned exchange market. It is calculated as an annual average based on monthly averages.
(IMF)

Female to male enrollments in primary and secondary school The ratio of female to male gross enrollment rates in primary and secondary school. (UNESCO Institute for Statistics)

Fertility rate, total The number of children that would be born to a woman if she were to live to the end of her childbearing years and bear children in accordance with current age-specific fertility rates.
(World Bank)

Fertilizer consumption The plant nutrients used per unit of arable land. It includes nitrogenous, potash, and phosphate fertilizers (including ground rock phosphate).

The time reference for fertilizer consumption is the crop year (July through June). (FAO)

Financing from abroad (obtained from nonresidents) and domestic financing (obtained from residents) The means by which a government provides financial resources to cover a budget deficit or allocates financial resources arising from a budget surplus. Includes all government liabilities—other than those for currency issues or demand, time, or savings deposits with government—or claims on others held by government, and changes in government holdings of cash and deposits. Excludes government guarantees of the debt of others. (IMF)

Food production index Covers food crops that are considered edible and that contain nutrients. Coffee and tea are excluded because, although edible, they have no nutritive value. (FAO)

Foreign direct investment, net inflows Net inflows of investment to acquire a lasting management interest (10 percent or more of voting stock) in an enterprise operating in an economy other than that of the investor. It is the sum of equity capital, reinvestment of earnings, other long-term capital, and short-term capital as shown in the balance of payments. (IMF)

Forest area Land under natural or planted stands of trees, whether productive or not. (FAO)

Freshwater resources Total renewable resources in the country and river flows from other countries. (World Resources Institute)

Freshwater withdrawals, annual Total water withdrawals, not counting evaporation losses from storage basins but including water from desalination plants in countries where they are a significant source. Withdrawal data are for single years between 1980 and 2000. Withdrawals can exceed 100 percent of total renewable resources where extraction from nonrenewable aquifers or desalination plants is considerable or where there is significant water reuse. (World Resources Institute)

Gross capital formation (commonly called 'investment') Outlays on additions to the fixed assets of the economy, net of changes in the level of inventories, and net acquisitions of valuables. Fixed assets include land improvements (fences, ditches, drains, and so on); plant, machinery, and equipment purchases; and the construction of roads, railways, dwellings, and the like. (World Bank, OECD, UN)

Gross domestic product (GDP) The sum of gross value added by all resident producers in the economy plus any product taxes (less subsidies) not included in the value of the products. It is calculated using purchaser prices and without deductions for the depreciation of fabricated assets or for the depletion and degradation of natural resources. (World Bank)

Gross domestic product (GDP) per capita Gross domestic product divided by midyear population. (World Bank)

Gross national income (GNI) Gross domestic product (GDP) plus net receipts of primary income (compensation of employees and property income) from abroad. Data are converted to dollars using the World Bank Atlas method. (World Bank)

Gross national income (GNI) per capita Gross national income divided by midyear population. (World Bank)

Gross national income (GNI), PPP Gross national income converted to international dollars using purchasing power parity rates. An international dollar has the same purchasing power over GNI as a US dollar has in the United States. (World Bank)

Heavily Indebted Poor Countries (HIPC) Initiative A program of official creditors designed to relieve the poorest, most heavily indebted countries of their debt to certain multilateral creditors, including the World Bank and IMF. (World Bank)

High-income economies Those with a gross national income (GNI) per capita of $10,726 or more in 2005.

HIV, adults and children living with All people with HIV infection, whether or not they have developed symptoms of AIDS. Adults are defined as those aged 15 and over and children as aged 0–14. (UNAIDS)

HIV, adult prevalence of The proportion of

people aged 15–49 who are infected with HIV. (UNAIDS)

Immunization rate, measles, child Percentage of children aged 12–23 months who received vaccination for measles before 12 months or at any time before the survey. A child is considered adequately immunized against measles after receiving one dose of vaccine.

Industry The output of the industrial sector corresponding to International Standard Industrial Classification (ISIC) divisions 40–45.

Interest payments Payments of interest on government debt—including long-term bonds, long-term loans, and other debt instruments—to both domestic and foreign residents. (World Bank)

Internet access Proportion of people with access to the world wide network. (International Telecommunication Union).

Land, arable Land under temporary crops (double-cropped areas are counted once), temporary meadows for mowing or for pasture, land under market or kitchen gardens, and land temporarily fallow. Land abandoned as a result of shifting cultivation is excluded. (FAO)

Land under cereal production Refers to harvested areas, although some countries report only sown or cultivated areas. (FAO)

Life expectancy at birth The number of years a newborn infant would live if prevailing patterns of mortality at the time of its birth were to stay the same throughout its life. (World Bank)

Low-income economies Those with a gross national income (GNI) per capita of $875 or less in 2005.

Malnutrition, underweight children, prevalence of The percentage of children under five whose weight for age is more than two standard deviations below the median for the international reference population aged 0–59 months. The reference population, adopted by the World Health Organization in 1983, is based on children from the United States, who are assumed to be well nourished. (WHO)

Manufacturing The output of industries corresponding to International Standard Industrial Classification (ISIC) divisions 15–37.

Merchandise trade The sum of merchandise exports and imports measured in current US dollars. Also referred to as trade in goods. (WTO)

Middle-income economies Those with a gross national income (GNI) per capita of more than $875 but less than $10,726 in 2005.

Migration, stock the number of people born in a country other than that in which they live. It includes refugees. (UNSD)

Mortality rate, infant The number of infants dying before reaching one year of age, per 1,000 live births in a given year. (Harmonized estimates of the World Health Organization, UNICEF, and the World Bank)

Mortality rate, children under-five The probability that a newborn baby will die before reaching age five, if subject to current age-specific mortality rates. The probability is expressed as a rate per 1,000. (Harmonized estimates of the World Health Organization, UNICEF, and the World Bank)

Mortality ratio, maternal The number of women who die from pregnancy-related causes during pregnancy and childbirth, per 100,000 live births. The data shown are modeled estimates based on an exercise by the World Health Organization, the United Nations Children's Fund, and the United Nations Population Fund. (WHO, UNICEF and UNFPA)

Nationally protected areas Totally or partially protected areas of at least 1,000 hectares that are designated as national parks, natural monuments, nature reserves or wildlife sanctuaries, protected landscapes or seascapes, or scientific reserves with limited public access. The data do not include sites protected under local or provincial law. Total land area is used to calculate the percentage of total area protected. (World Conservation Monitoring Centre)

Official Aid Grants and loans (net of repayments) that meet the criteria for official development assistance and are made to countries and territories in part II of the Development Assistance Committee's list of aid recipients. (OECD)

Official development assistance (ODA) Grants and loans (net of repayments of principal) that meet the Development Assistance Committee (DAC) definition of ODA and are made to developing countries and territories in Part I of the DAC's list of recipients. (OECD)

Official development assistance (ODA) provided for basic social services Aid provided for basic health, education, nutrition, and water and sanitation services as reported by Development Assistance Committee members. (OECD)

Particulate matter (PM10) Fine suspended particulates less than 10 microns in diameter that are capable of penetrating deep into the respiratory tract and causing significant health damage. (World Bank)

Permanent cropland Land cultivated with crops that occupy the land for long periods and need not be replanted after each harvest. It includes land under flowering shrubs, fruit trees, nut trees, and vines, but excludes land under trees grown for wood or timber. (FAO)

Phones, fixed lines and mobile phone subscribers Telephone mainlines connecting a customer's equipment to the public switched telephone network, and users of portable telephones who subscribe to a service that uses cellular technology to provide access to the network. (ITU)

Population, average annual growth rate The exponential rate of change in population for the period indicated. (World Bank)

Population, total Includes all residents regardless of legal status or citizenship—except for refugees not permanently settled in the country of asylum, who are generally considered part of the population of their country of origin. (World Bank)

Population below $1 a day The proportion of the population living on less than $1.08 a day at 1993 purchasing power parity prices. (World Bank)

Population below $2 a day The proportion of the population living on less than $2.15 a day at 1993 purchasing power parity prices. (World Bank)

Population density Midyear population divided by land area in square kilometers.

Population, rural Calculated as the difference between the total population and the urban population. (World Bank)

Population, urban The population of urban agglomerations—contiguous inhabited territories defined without regard to administrative boundaries. (World Bank)

Pregnant women receiving prenatal care The proportion of women attended at least once during pregnancy by skilled health personnel for reasons related to pregnancy. (UNICEF)

Primary completion rate The proportion of students completing the last year of primary school, calculated by taking the total number of students in the last grade of primary school, minus the number of repeaters in that grade, divided by the total number of children of official graduation age. (UNESCO Institute for Statistics)

Private capital flows, net Private debt flows including commercial bank lending, bonds, and other private credits; and nondebt flows including foreign direct investment and portfolio equity investment. (IMF)

Private participation in infrastructure Infrastructure projects in telecommunications, energy, transport, and water and sanitation that have reached financial closure and directly or indirectly serve the public. All investment (public and private) in projects in which a private company assumes the operating risk is included. (World Bank)

Property rights, lack of confidence in the courts to uphold The share of managers who do not agree with the statement: "I am confident that the judicial system will enforce my contractual and property rights in business disputes". (World Bank)

Purchasing power parity (PPP) conversion factor The number of units of a country's currency required to buy the same amount of goods and services in the domestic market as a US dollar would buy in the United States. (World Bank)

Services Corresponds to International Standard Industrial Classification (ISIC) divisions

50–99. Value added from this sector is derived as a residual (from GDP less agriculture and industry) and may not properly reflect the output of services, including banking and financial services.

Tariff, simple mean The unweighted average of the effectively applied rates for all products subject to tariffs. (World Bank, UNCTAD, WTO)

Trade As used in this book, trade refers to the two-way flow of exports and imports of goods (merchandise trade) and services (service trade).

Treated bednets, use of The proportion of children aged 0–59 months who slept under an insecticide-impregnated bednet the night before the survey. (UNICEF)

Tuberculosis, incidence of The estimated number of new pulmonary, smear-positive, and extrapulmonary tuberculosis cases. (WHO)

Unpaid family worker Unpaid workers who work in a business operated by a relative and live in the same household. (ILO)

Unofficial payments to get things done: Average value of gifts or informal payments to public officials to 'get things done' with regard to customs, taxes, licenses, regulations, services, etc. The values shown indicate a percentage of annual sales. (World Bank).

Value added The net output of an industry after adding up all outputs and subtracting intermediate inputs. The industrial origin of value added is determined by the International Standard Industrial Classification (ISIC) revision 3.

Water source, access to an improved The share of the population with reasonable access to water from an improved source, such as a household connection, public standpipe, borehole, protected well or spring, or rainwater collection. Unimproved sources include vendors, tanker trucks, and unprotected wells and springs. Reasonable access is defined as the availability of at least 20 liters a person per day from a source within one kilometer of the dwelling. (WHO)

Women in parliament The percentage of parliamentary seats in a single or lower chamber occupied by women. (IPU)

Women's participation rate in the labor force The proportion of the female population aged 15–64 that is economically active. (ILO)

Workers' remittances and compensation of employees, received Current transfers by migrant workers and wages and salaries earned by nonresident workers. (World Bank and IMF)

World Bank Atlas method A conversion factor used by the World Bank to convert national currency units to US dollars at prevailing exchange rates, adjusted for inflation and averaged over three years. The purpose is to reduce the effect of exchange rate fluctuations in the cross-country comparison of national incomes.

Data sources

The indicators presented in this Atlas are compiled by international agencies and by public and private organizations, usually on the basis of survey data or administrative statistics obtained from national governments. The principal source of each indicator is given in parentheses following the indicator definition.

The World Bank publishes these and many other statistical series in *World Development Indicators,* available in print, CD-ROM, and online. Excerpts from this atlas, additional information about sources, definitions, and statistical methods, and suggestions for further reading are available at www.worldbank.org/data.

Data notes and symbols

The data in this book are for the most recent year unless otherwise noted.
• Growth rates are proportional changes from the previous year unless otherwise noted.
• Regional aggregates include data for low- and middle-income economies only.
• Figures in italics indicate data for years or periods other than those specified.

Data are shown for economies with populations greater than 30,000 or less if they are members of the World Bank. The term *country* (used interchangeably with *economy*) does not imply political independence or official recognition by the World Bank but refers to any economy for which the authorities report separate social or economic statistics.

The regional groupings of countries include only low- and middle-income economies. For the income groups, every economy is classified as low income, middle income or high income. Low-income economies are those with a GNI per capita of $875 or less in 2005. Middle-income economies are those with a GNI per capita of $876 or more but less than $10,725. Lower-middle-income and upper-middle income economies are separated at a GNI per capita of $3,465. High-income economies are those with a GNI per capita of $10,726 or more.

Symbols used in data table

.. means that data are not available or that aggregates cannot be calculated because of missing data.
0 or 0.0 means zero or less than half the unit shown.
$ means current US dollars.
The methods used to calculate regional and income group aggregates are denoted by:
m (median), s (simple total), t (total including estimates for missing data), u (unweighted average), and w (weighted average).

Abbreviations

CPIA	Country Policy and Institutional Assessment	ODA	Official Development Assistance
DAC	Development Assistance Committee of the Organisation for Economic Co-operation and Development	OECD	Organisation for Economic Co-operation and Development
DHS	Demographic and Health Surveys	PPI	Private Participation in Infrastructure
FAO	Food and Agriculture Organization of the United Nations	PPP	Purchasing Power Parity
		UN	United Nations
FDI	Foreign Direct Investment	UNAIDS	Joint United Nations Programme on HIV/AIDS
GDP	Gross Domestic Product	UNDP	United Nations Development Programme
GNI	Gross National Income	UNEP	United Nations Environment Programme
HIPC	Heavily Indebted Poor Countries	UNESCO	United Nations Educational, Scientific and Cultural Organization
ICT	Information and Communications Technology		
IDA	International Development Association	UNFPA	United Nations Population Fund
ILO	International Labour Organization	UNICEF	United Nations Children's Fund
IMF	International Monetary Fund	UNIFEM	United Nations Development Fund for Women
ITU	International Telecommunication Union	WCMC	World Conservation Monitoring Centre
MDGs	Millennium Development Goals	WDI	World Development Indicators
MDRI	Multilateral Debt Relief Initiative	WHO	World Health Organization

For more information

Visit www.worldbank.org/data to find out more about these and other publications:
• *World Development Indicators* and **WDI Online** The World Bank's premier compilation of data about development. This atlas complements *World Development Indicators* by providing a geographical view of pertinent data.
• *Global Development Finance* and **GDF Online** The World Bank's comprehensive compilation of data on external debt and financial flows.
• *African Development Indicators* The World Bank's most detailed collection of data on Africa, available in one volume.
• *Global Economic Prospects* The World Bank's publication that outlines steps that rich and poor countries can take to accelerate growth rates and poverty reduction.
• **www.developmentgoals.org** The Millennium Development Goals and the data and indicators required to track progress toward them.
• **www.paris21.org** The PARIS21 Consortium and how it promotes evidence-based policymaking and monitoring.
• **www.worldbank.org/data/tas** Tools and advice for statistical capacity building in developing countries.
• **www.worldbank.org/data/icp** The International Comparison Program and progress on the 2003–2005 round.

Index

Note: page numbers in **bold** refer to maps, page numbers in *italics* refer to information presented in graphs and tables.